MIDDLESEX VOL II

Edited by Sarah Lester

First published in Great Britain in 1998 by
POETRY NOW YOUNG WRITERS
1-2 Wainman Road, Woodston,
Peterborough, PE2 7BU
Telephone (01733) 230748

All Rights Reserved

Copyright Contributors 1998

HB ISBN 0 75430 211 3
SB ISBN 0 75430 212 1

FOREWORD

With over 63,000 entries for this year's Cosmic competition, it has proved to be our most demanding editing year to date.

We were, however, helped immensely by the fantastic standard of entries we received, and, on behalf of the Young Writers team, thank you.

Cosmic Middlesex Vol II is a tremendous reflection on the writing abilities of 10 & 11 year old children, and the teachers who have encouraged them must take a great deal of credit.

We hope that you enjoy reading *Cosmic Middlesex Vol II* and that you are impressed with the variety of poems and style with which they are written, giving an insight into the minds of young children and what they think about the world today.

CONTENTS

Dean Barnett	1
Keshina Bouri	1
Louise Wynter	2

Barham Primary School

Kaushal Pindoria	3
S Anuraj	4
Sarah Ishaq	4
Leila Chauhan	5
Fiona Gair	5
Kalpa Shah	5

Brookside Primary School

Sobia Mughal	6
Jennifer Hale Lamb	7
James Burke	7
Gordon Hughes	8

Buckingham College Prep School

Sujan Patel	8
Chrishan Tailor	9
Kishan Vekeria	9
Jaysal Patel	10
Shirish Patel	11
Bimal Sualy	12
Dominic Beeput	13
Kavi Kotecha	13
Amar Shah	14
Ranjeet Johal	14
Krupesh Patel	15
Arjun Anand	15
Mehool Mistry	16
Kishan Patel	16

James Elton	17
Bhaumik Patel	17
Dipesh Virji	18
Dev Jadva	18

Buxlow Preparatory School

Elise Goldin	19
Teshome Dennis	19

Coston Primary School

Hannah Young	20
Aman Bhatti	20
Elanor Speight	21
Gemma Giles-Walker	21
Shallinder Singh Bhogal	22
Gurveer Vasir	22
Jasmin Rodgman	23
Amy Johnson	23
Mark Ahmet	24
Lucky Sidhu	24
Rebecca Taylor	25
Fatima Mirza	25
Madiha Rashid	26
Adel Toms	26
Larisa Williams	27
Peter R Seward	27
Emman Bhati	28
Thomas Wood	28
Leena Dodhia	29
Gary Johnson	29

Collis Primary School

Robert Lupton	30
Martyn Davies	30
Lorraine Kent	31
Mark Smith	31
Philip Linter	32
Rachel Ramsay	32

B J Pratt	33
Emma Hibbert	33
Freddie Ridge	34
Neil Kotecha	34
Scott McKenzie	35
Thomas Stell	35
Fergus McIntosh	36
Lauren Ray	36
Kirsty Ivison	37
Jared David Short	37
Olivia Laura Nixson	38
Gregory Unsworth	38
Samuel Manning	39
Jemma Holdaway	40
Thomas Caldwell	40
Cait Orton	41
Mungo Coyne	41
Carla Jane Holding	42
Victoria Howe	42
Emma Knight	43
Alex Cox	43
Francesca Rose Gray	44
Aisha Krupska	45
Naomi Kay	46

Deanesfield Primary School

Sarah-Jane Sexton	46
Rosie Biddlecombe	47
Yousef Khalifa	47
Thomas Kebble	48
Kurt McKenna	48
Kirsty Treadwell	49
Jack Hann	49
David Newton	50
Billy Brown	50
Stephen Mooney	51
Tommy Fountain	51
Matthew Molloy	52

Lee Harvison	52
Aiysha Patel	53
Verity Bristow	53
Thomas Groves	54
Ian Smith	54
Kelly Tiretis	55
Kelly Eustice	55
Christopher Marnoch	56
Gemma Warman	56
Hayley Casey	57
Georgina Lanning	57
Lauren Scott	58
Bradley Gilbert	58
Alex MacDonald	59
Charlotte Smith	59
Robert Macfarlaine	60
Anthony Gourlay	60
Daniel O'Brien	61
Dawn Wood	61
James McMillan	62
Hayley Greaves	62
Katie-Jane Sams	63
Erhyn Wingrove-Owens	63
Zoê Cornish	64
Stacey Beard	64
James Lanning	65
Louise Clarke	65

Elmgrove Middle School

Nisha Shah	66
Nicola Bubenzer	66
Bijal Savadia	67
Natasha Kwaskowska	68
Kishan Joshi	69

Frithwood Primary School

Rebecca Singer	69
Peter Shelton	70

Jack Bennington	70
Antony Bronson	71
Andrew Sinclair	72
Alfie Mancini	72
Pagan Leigh Toland	73
Lianne Winter	73
Louisa Willoughby	74
Alice Whalley	75
Jonathan Parker	75
Rachael Steele	76
Cassy O'Neill	76
Amira Tejani	76
Shruti Patel	77

George Spicer Primary School

Alison Powell	77
Melissa Ann Brown	78
Daniel Chapman	79
Allison Edwards	79
Catherine Bradly	80
Ashley Louise Wright	80
Joanna Costa	81
Tom Hall	81
Holly Kalogirou	82
Samantha Rayner	83

Harmondsworth Primary School

Kirsty Lipscombe	83
Rachel Dent	84
Victoria Simmonds	84
Sophie Price	85

Hythe School

Charlotte Connolly	85
Sharon Appleton	86
Jason Townsend	86
Stacey Lynn Hill	87
Katie Anne Harding	88

Stephanie Dowsett	88
Lee Garland	89
Thomas James Flanagan	89

Hayes Park Primary School

Michelle Condon	90
Lauren Coyle	91
Amandeep Shihn	92
Jenni Bull	93

Lady Bankes Junior School

Jessica Brooks	93
Jack Lisi	94
Jamie Campbell	94
Katrina Zimmerman	95
Lois Beaven	95
Bradley Thomas	96
Matthew West	96
Laura Zimmerman	97
Joe Perry	97
Epu Choudhury	98
Kate Louise Balkin	99
Stephanie Alam	99
Eileen Chapman	100
Lisa-Marie	100
Chris Simmonds	101
Jennifer Hanrahan	101

Islamia Primary School

Rabiah Chaudhry	102

Longfield Middle School

Paul Mant	103
Mitin Dattani	103
Ashley Strawbridge	104
Katie Leahey	105

Lavender Primary School
Clare Molloy	105
Nikki Webb	106
Chaemil Rbyn Goodfellow	106
Natalie Kaye	107
Emma Bedford	107

Pinner Park Middle School
Richard Chapman	108
Jinisha Patel	108
Paul Murray	109
Ban Nasar	109
Komal Mistry	110
Donna Phipp	110
Laura Nicholson	111
Aimee Oram	111
Yusuf Aleem	112

Raglan Junior School
Rose Dykins	113
Sarah Boyes	113

St Christopher's School
Sam Lindsay	114
Ben Tucker	114
Ross Kemp	115
Alexandra Doonan	116
Rebecca Levy	117
Lakshman Harendran	118
Kathleen Moloney	118
Nico Dontas	119
Nadine Higgin	120
Samina Karimbhai	121

St Mary's RC Primary School
- Joanna Smith — 122
- Sharon Entsua-Mensah — 122
- Katie Bermingham — 123
- Sam Hyman — 124

St Matthew's CE Primary School
- Laura Moody — 124
- Thomas Alner-Newns — 125
- Farha Ahmed — 126
- Sophia Tremenheere — 126
- Carl Perryman — 127

Suffolks Primary School
- Lauren Johnston — 128
- Charley Gudgeon — 128
- Shanie Partridge — 129
- Shaun Howlett — 129
- Alex Massey — 129

Springfield Primary School
- Elizabeth Proctor — 130
- Daniel Fair — 130
- Nourdine Arsalane — 131
- Quynh Vo — 132
- Chloe Wall — 132
- Loan Kim Thi Truong — 133
- Charlotte Dudfield — 134
- Lee Cornwall — 134
- Andraé Michael Barrow — 135
- Lauren Wadley — 135
- David Howard — 136

Trafalgar Junior School
- Polly Checker — 136
- Kathryn Sibley — 137
- Jess Purdue — 137

Tudor Primary School
- Baljinder Sekhon — 138
- Nisha Mohammed — 138
- Kulvinder Dhaliwal — 139
- Karina Atwal — 139
- Jasbinder Nijjar — 140
- Suchet Bhamra — 140
- Navjit Singha — 141
- Anju Ganger — 141
- Kiranjit Gill — 142
- Dale Thomas — 142
- Nudrat Rana — 142
- Sukhdev Shah — 143
- Sahra Handule — 143
- Hushpreet Dhaliwal — 144
- Lale Saleque — 144
- Ashil Waheed — 145

Warrender School
- Gurpreet Mudhar — 145
- Alex Bulfin — 146
- Virginia Anne Pilborough — 146
- Michael Meehan — 147
- Nathan Mayer — 148
- Bernice Pike — 148
- James O'Connor — 149
- Charley Cox — 149
- Patrick Morris — 150
- Holly Ryan — 150
- Emma Frankal — 151
- Sian Roberts — 151
- Aminur Rahman — 152
- Nina Chambers — 152
- Christina Western — 153
- Grace Rumball — 154

Wembley Manor Junior School
Shyam Pandya	154
Neelam Amin	155
Yannick Wood	155
Caroline Wyszynski	156
Liza Wilkinson	156
Vishal Sedani	157
Shalini Parjan	158
Nilesh Sikotra	158
Rajiv Wijesuriya	159
Cheri Savary	159
Amy Gilbey	160
Mark Roach	160
Kyriacos Papasavva	161
Vijay Tailor	161
Sherida Blenman	162

THE POEMS

TRANSPORT

Travelling on a train,
flying on a plane,
driving in a car, that way it seems so far.

The train track clatters
and the plane will roar,
the car is boring so we all snore.

I've got to go to school,
I'm really in a rush,
the car has broken down, so I think I'll take the bus.

I've got to go camping,
It's what they call a hike,
I don't think I'll walk
but I think I'll take my bike.

Travelling on a train,
flying on a plane,
driving in a car, that way it seems so far.

Dean Barnett

RAIN, THUNDER, LIGHTNING

Rain, thunder, lightning
Different kinds of weather.
Pitter, patter goes the rain
Bang! Bang! Goes the thunder.
Crash! Crash! Goes the lightning.

Rain, thunder, lightning.

Keshina Bouri (8)

WILDLIFE IN DANGER

Ten powerful gorillas
In a stooped position
'Ashtrays!' shouted the poachers
They've completed their mission.

Nine long blue whales
Cruising on the sea
Captured for performance
For all of us to see.

Eight plump seals
Plodding across the sand
An oil tanker hits the rocks
The oil pollutes the land.

Seven slow moving turtles
Taking their time
Their shells are valuable souvenirs
Worth more than a dime.

Six brightly striped tigers
Striding proudly around in the heat
Bang! Go the poachers' guns
Their skin is walked upon by many feet.

Five round barn owls
Nesting in the roof is their zone
Farmers knock down their hay barns
Now they've lost their homes.

Four grey elephants
Swinging their trunks at ease
Poachers chop off their ivory
For more piano keys.

Three red admiral butterflies
Feeding on plant nectar
Plants have been sprayed with insecticide
Around two hundred hectares.

Two bushy-tailed foxes
Sharp and cunning
Hunters with dogs and horns
To stop the fox running.

One timid dormouse
Hiding in a hawthorn bush safe and sound
Farmers cut down their hedges
Now open to predators where it can be found.

No animals left
What have we done?
No more wildlife
For the next generation.

Louise Wynter (11)

ONE WICKED WITCH

One wicked witch won a war
Two tricky tarantulas talking to each other
Three tremendous trees trying to grow taller
Four fantastic fish following friendly females
Five ferocious families fishing in the sea
Six sticky sticks standing on stones
Seven slippery spanners spelling supper
Eight enormous elves eating eggs
Nine nosy nans having a nap
Ten tasty tomatoes tickling toes.

Kaushal Pindoria (10)
Barham Primary School

My New Year's Resolutions

I will never throw the cat out of the window.
Or put a frog in my sister's bed.
I will not tie my brother's shoelaces together.
Nor jump from the roof of Dad's shed.
I will not remember my aunt's next birthday.
And tidy my room once a week.
I will make the kitchen pipe leak.
I will not moan at Mum's cooking (Ugh! Smelly fish fingers again!)
If I kick or swear . . .
I'll always say I don't care.
I will not pick my nose any more (not really because I like the taste!)

S Anuraj (10)
Barham Primary School

Flowers

Flowers, flowers everywhere,
Bluebells here,
Snowdrops there,
My friend has pansies.
And they don't give you any diseases,
I love flowers,
The smell lasts for hours.

Sarah Ishaq (10)
Barham Primary School

BLUE

Blue is the hot summer's sky,
Blue is the crashing waves in an ocean,
Blue is the messy paint palette,
Blue is the fluent singing of a blue tit,
Blue is the gentle petals of a clematis,
Blue is the cold water in my sink.

Leila Chauhan (10)
Barham Primary School

BLUE

Blue is the rough roaring of the sea
Blue is the blue messy paint all over me
Blue is the sweet singing of a blue bird
Blue is the rushing sound of the river
Blue is the sound of a blueberry being squashed.

Fiona Gair (10)
Barham Primary School

WATER

The beautiful water falling from the sky.
The sweet water falling onto my tongue.
The water is as clear as crystal.
The water has a sweet flavour.
The water makes us stay alive.

Kalpa Shah (10)
Barham Primary School

THE MEDITERRANEAN SEA

Around the island of Crete,
There lies a cool, calm crystal clear sea,
Where all sea creatures meet
For a cup of cold sea tea!

Then all of a sudden,
There's a murky, monstrous moan,
And out pops a shark,
And says in a deep, gruff tone;

'Well, well, well what have we here?'
The sneaky, silver shark boasted
To his friends under the pier.

'Ahhhh!' jabbered the fishes,
As they swam away and away.
Until they came to the seabed
And they lay there
As quiet as seven, sneaky mice.

They lay there for months and years.
Until those corrupt, cruel criminals
Escaped from under the piers.
And never came back for years!

        But do you know where they went?

Sobia Mughal (10)
Brookside Primary School

THE NORTH ATLANTIC OCEAN

The fierce, frightening, ferocious, frantic North Atlantic Ocean.
She is a silk scarf, swallowing shoals of fish!

The dolphin is swift, sensible, soft and sleek.
To swim around the world it would take a week.
A dolphin wouldn't hurt a human soul.
But a shark would probably eat one whole!

Throughout the extensive ocean.
They're making mystic, magic, motions.
The lazy, lonely, long-nosed swordfish,
Lies on the comfortable seabed.

The friendly killer whale swims in the deep, dark, drowning ocean.
But why do you think that it's called a killer whale?

Jennifer Hale Lamb (11)
Brookside Primary School

DREAM OF A TEACHER

You asked me, what did I dream?
I dreamt I became a teacher.
You asked me, why did I want to become a teacher?
I would like to help children learn.
You asked me, why did I want to help children learn?
To give children a better education.
You asked me, why did I want to give children a better education?
So they can get a good job.
You asked me, why did I want them to have a good job?
So they could earn lots of money.

James Burke (11)
Brookside Primary School

FANTASTIC FRANCE!

The Eiffel Tower doesn't end,
Paris' tower stops at top, middle and end.
Scream, shout, screech and scare!
Don't be surprised if you see a bear.

Disneyland is like a dream.
I'll know if you're on Space Mountain because I'll hear you scream!
Disney's theme park is perfected in every way.
It's hard to get tickets but what a holiday!
Do you think you would want to stay?

The Frenchman's fabulous fancy fromage feeds foreigners.
They eat and drink like lightweight scavengers!
The crêpes are stingrays, folded with jam and sugar in.
If you buy one,
I doubt you'll throw it in the bin!
Their French bread's a favourite food,
The way French eat, you can't look rude!

Gordon Hughes (11)
Brookside Primary School

SPORTS DAY

Sports Day is fun,
We all have a run,
We throw a javelin,
And a shot-put,
We jump into sand,
And over a pole,
Sports Day is fun,
We all have a bun.

Sujan Patel (10)
Buckingham College Prep School

MY COLOURS

White, white reminds me of light,
Like the moon in the night.

Green, green reminds me of runner beans,
Dissolving in the steam.

Red, red reminds me of the cover of my bed,
Whilst I lie down on my head.

Blue, blue reminds me of my loo,
In which I have tissue.

Gold, gold makes you bold,
So I am told.

Chrishan Tailor (10)
Buckingham College Prep School

SNOW

I'm skiing through the city,
I feel angels around my head,
I skied into a bin,
I went all soggy,
Children playing in the snow,
Through the window,
Is a stuffed turkey,
Luscious!
My heart melts.

Kishan Vekeria (10)
Buckingham College Prep School

TIGER

I was prowling and snarling,
Having some fun,
And also running around.

When there in the bushes,
I heard a rustle,
So I hid in the grass.

And when I knew what it was,
Time to jump,
I did.

But to my horror I saw,
Two people with a gun,
And before I could guard myself,
They shot a bullet at me.

And all I could see were two people,
All dressed in green and all I could hear,
Were the words 'Get him.'

When I woke up,
I saw to my dismay,
I was in a cage.

People were laughing and sniggering at me,
And one man called me his pet,
I snarled and roared,
I bit the cage,
And tried to scare the people,
But all I could do was sit and stare.

Jaysal Patel (10)
Buckingham College Prep School

TEN SAD TEACHERS

Ten sad teachers out to dine,
One got left there,
Then there were nine.
Nine sad teachers used as bait,
One got caught,
Then there were eight.
Eight sad teachers looking at heaven,
One got sent there,
Then there were seven.
Seven sad teachers eating chips,
One choked,
Then there were six.
Six sad teachers going for a dive,
One drowned,
Then there were five.
Five sad teachers on a walk on the moor,
One got lost,
Then there were four.
Four sad teachers going on a spree,
One got kicked,
Then there were three.
Three sad teachers going to the loo,
One got flushed,
Then there were two.
Two sad teachers eating a bun,
One got poisoned,
Then there was one.
One sad teacher looking up a gun,
Out came the bullet,
Then there was none.

Shirish Patel (11)
Buckingham College Prep School

MY TEACHERS AT SCHOOL

I left nursery at three
Came to Buckingham at four to learn more
English, maths, science and all.

Mr Murphy teaches maths
Areas, fractions, decimals and angles
Gets me in a tangle with the rest!

For English it is Miss McRae
We learn it day by day
Comprehensions, spellings and essays!

Mr Evans teaches science and games
One we learn, one we play
Experiments at which we are amazed and goals that we gain!

Mr Cooper comes for French
We are waiting on our bench!
Un, deux, trois, quatre, cinq, up we go in rank!

Here comes Mr Smith
Whom we love to be with
As headmaster of the school
He teaches us to obey the rules!

It's been seven years at the school
And I will be leaving soon!
With all the knowledge I have gained
I am sure not to fail!

Bimal Sualy (10)
Buckingham College Prep School

COLOURS

What is silver? It is a gun,
which shot a bullet at the sun.

What is black? It is a cat,
in a witch's hat.

What is silver? It is rain,
which comes flying to the brain.

What is black? It is ink,
when it falls in your eyes you blink.

What is silver? It is a ring,
you see a bee, it might sting.

What is black? It is space,
a chimney sweep has a black face.

Dominic Beeput (10)
Buckingham College Prep School

MY BUDGIE

My budgie has beautiful wings.
Blue with little black spots.

He has an orange beak
And two beautiful nostrils.

His little pink feet walking away.
    My budgie!

Kavi Kotecha (11)
Buckingham College Prep School

My Favourite Events

Sports Day, Swimming Gala, Summer Fair,
These sort of things should be everywhere!

Cricket matches, trip to the zoo,
What else ought we to do?

Clubs, Animal Ark!
What's the point of going to the park?

The army's just about to come in,
I'm so excited, I don't know where I've been!

The summer BBQ,
Is every year for you!

Amar Shah (10)
Buckingham College Prep School

Silver

I like silver
It reminds me of the moon on a cold night.
Of swords clashing,
And knights dashing.
Silver is bright,
Romantic,
Cold,
And light.

Silver is a swan's reflection in the water.

Ranjeet Johal (11)
Buckingham College Prep School

A Life Of A Sad Animal

I'm an animal sad and alone,
Standing in readiness for my show,
I'm taken out into a field like a subject,
I was thrown about like a piece of rubbish,
I was put in a cage,
I could not move while others could
I'm a living thing too,
I was pushed against a lot of wires,
My back got sore and cold,
How could my owner never notice me?

The money greedy man was an executor,
He made my throat hurt and my body warm,
I got thrown on sharp blades of grass,
My back felt like a hundred swords had stabbed me,
As I got up I danced,
I felt foolish.

Krupesh Patel (11)
Buckingham College Prep School

Chocolate

I like the chocolate stars
because they are yummy for your tummy.
You can get different flavours:
chocolate, strawberry and vanilla.
I like them because it is like
eating the stars from the sky.

Arjun Anand (10)
Buckingham College Prep School

The Sun

The sun reminds me of myself
Lying there on the beach on a
Nice sunny day.

It reminds me of,
Sunflowers growing in the garden,
Slowly but nicely.

On a hot, sunny and joyful day,
It reminds me of my friends and I
Playing football,
On the school playground.

Mehool Mistry (10)
Buckingham College Prep School

Sunny

The sun makes me hot,
Really hot,
It melts me down,
Like a broken heart,
It reminds me of the golden sand,
Bright, gleaming and shiny,
On the beautiful beach,
And the tall green palm trees,
Leaning over the sea.
Flowers bloom to their full size,
And people swim through the crystal clear blue sea.

Kishan Patel (10)
Buckingham College Prep School

IT IS VERY SUNNY

In the summer it is very sunny,
When it is sunny the sun is out,
And it is normally very hot,
The sun is burning hot.

Lots of children play in the park,
When it is a very sunny day.
Lots of families go to the seaside,
In the summer.

It is very sunny at midday,
But it gets colder in the evening.
It is not hot at night at all,
At night it is very cold.

James Elton (11)
Buckingham College Prep School

WHEN THE SNOW FALLS

When the snow falls,
The city looks as if a white sheet has been dropped on it.
Children happily throw snowballs at each other.
In pairs people ice skate.
Snowflakes in the morning slowly drift down and touch
                                      the ground slowly.
Skiers ski down the mountains in delight.
People shiver in the cold winter's breeze.
Children sleight down a hill happily.
Some people slip on the cold December ice.

Bhaumik Patel (10)
Buckingham College Prep School

THE SNOW

The month of December,
I shall always remember.

Because I cannot stay away,
From the icy bay.

Through the door with my sleigh
Out, of course, to play.

I can feel snowflakes,
As I can hear screeching brakes.

My day has ended,
The snow has descended.

Dipesh Virji (10)
Buckingham College Prep School

THE MOST FUN DAY EVER

It's Christmas Day.
It's Christmas Day.
Let's have a gay day.
Open the presents.
And put out the cards.
Stuff the turkey and
Have a great laugh.

Dev Jadva (11)
Buckingham College Prep School

MY GRANDMA

My grandma is very fussy,
And chats, chats, *chats!* For ages,
She is always asking this and that,
And when I ask for one potato
She says 'Have another.'

My grandma is the greatest cook,
Apple pie and ice-cream, 'Yum, yum!'
Fishballs, homemade chips,
My grandma's famous chicken soup,
My grandma will make me fat!

My grandma gives me fun times,
Walking to the duck pond,
Rose garden and park,
And when I have some work to do,
'Thank god' she lets me work in peace!

Elise Goldin (10)
Buxlow Preparatory School

TONIGHT AT NOON

The Titanic will be raised from the seabed
Princess Diana will be saved
Adolf Hitler and Winston Churchill will be friends
War will not be a common word in the world
And there is another galaxy out there in space.

Teshome Dennis (10)
Buxlow Preparatory School

THE RIVER

Swans on the water
sailing by,
Ducks and birds swiftly fly,
Fieldmice in the reeds,
The farmer sowing his seeds.
The fat, wet water-vole,
Jumping out of its soggy hole.
The gushing rain comes
and makes the crops grow,
The wide stream of water
gently flows.

Hannah Young (10)
Coston Primary School

BLUE

The sun in the sky.
My fountain pen which I got for Christmas.
Water that swirls round the Earth.
Eyes of my friend.
Icy lands of the North Pole.
Clothes that I wear to parties.
My front door of my house.
The jeans I got for my birthday.
Electric from the electric socket.
My snooker ball on my table.

Aman Bhatti (10)
Coston Primary School

COLOURS

Purple is a colour for royalty
Handsome and huge and really mighty.

Yellow is a bright colour
the colour of the sun,
It shines with all its might
until the moon comes out at night.

Green is a sign saying 'Go.'
A green man lets you cross the road,
it changes the colours of the traffic lights.
It's the colour of nature, trees and wildlife.

Grey is a boring colour,
it reminds me of the dull days we sometimes have,
It's the colour of a cat that camouflages itself against a grey hat.

Elanor Speight (10)
Coston Primary School

GREEN

As I run through the thick blades of grass it tickles my legs.
My bedroom wallpaper with a pretty border round it.
The leaves in springtime with lovely blossoms on them.
My pencil case as I put my pens in it.
My mum's eye make-up as I watch her put it on.
At the end of the day I pick the grass and then fall asleep.

Gemma Giles-Walker (11)
Coston Primary School

TEACHERS

Our teachers at school are as mad as can be,
They get out their pencils and start drawing on me,
I wonder if I'm going a bit crazy or loony
I'm not amused but I think they are confused.
Our teachers at school are as crazy as can be,
They all spill their tea on some students like me.
Our books are stained with coffee and tea and
On top of that they throw chewing gum at me.
I think about it every day,
Does the headmaster think it's OK?

Shallinder Singh Bhogal (10)
Coston Primary School

BLUE

As I look up in the sky,
The twinkling stars catch my eye,
The aeroplanes fly by in the sky,
Zooming here and there.
As I look out of my window
The misty moon shines down on me.
As winter comes snow falls down,
The cold breeze falls through me.
The look of the bluebells,
Makes me feel happy.

Gurveer Vasir (10)
Coston Primary School

CATS!

Cats can be slinky and slick if you've seen,
Some can be dirty, some can be clean.
He has a tail, fat and fluffy,
She has a face, pale and puffy.
They can be naughty, mischievous, bad!
Happy, lonesome, stupid, sad!
Most cats are very, very attractive,
Maybe you find some strangely inactive.
You might find cat hair on the mat,
Probably in your auntie's new hat!
I can tell you, just listen to me,
This is one big aristocracy!

Jasmin Rodgman (10)
Coston Primary School

TIME

Time ticks away
Leaving you behind.
Clocks, watches
Are always on my mind.
Second by second
My life drains away.
Minute by minute
Day by day.

Amy Johnson (11)
Coston Primary School

GREEN

It is the grass in summertime,
The leaf on the young autumn tree,
A golf course that's just been cut,
The soft and gentle grass below,
A Get Well Card for your friend,
A dinosaur a long time ago,
A pen I got for my birthday,
Some vegetables in the garden,
My dad's new bike,
My mum's new car,
A city light on its own,
A science and geography book box.

Mark Ahmet (10)
Coston Primary School

HAVE YOU SEEN MY FOOLISH DOG?

Have you seen my foolish dog?
The one that barks at cars,
And hates a bath?
I bet you he's trying to get the meat which
Is on the top shelf right now!
He may be foolish, he may be bad,
I would never swap him for all the treasures in the world.

Lucky Sidhu (11)
Coston Primary School

MY AUNT ESMERELDA

My Aunt Esmerelda,
nature is her laugh,
My Aunt Esmerelda, animals she greets.
Every rainy evening, she will
go out in the wet rain,
and lift her head to Mother Nature,
as she would do time and time again.
She loves the feeling of her matted long hair,
Tangled and dripping, soaking in the rain.
Her long dress trailing behind her.
She takes her goats out of the yard,
And feeds them with joy,
Knowing the sun is off its guard
and setting in the summer sky.
And she gets too old and has to die.
I will lift my head and hear Mother Nature's cry.

Rebecca Taylor (10)
Coston Primary School

REST IN PEACE

She lay there sound asleep.
Asleep for ever with her world of mysteries.
Many secrets still not told.
Many things still not done.
All alone from now, she lay there
Looking as pale as dawn.
Rest in peace for ever now.

Fatima Mirza (10)
Coston Primary School

The Roaring Waterfall

Splish, splash
Lish, lish,
Shliff, shliff
The water
rushing, crashing
down the waterfall
Slashing, crashing,
Swishing, swashing
down the stones
The big hard rocks
roaring, falling,
down in a fast rush
down the river into the sea.
The faster it goes
The harder it splashes.
Swish, swash,
Slish, slash.

Madiha Rashid (10)
Coston Primary School

In The Rain

Drip drop
Splish splash
People playing in puddles
Blip blop plip plop
the rain trickling
down.

Adel Toms (10)
Coston Primary School

KILLING SHARK

Red, raging, killing shark
Horrible, hardly any feelings.
Killing people all the time
He doesn't care about anyone but himself,
Oh my gosh look at the time, I've got to kill someone by nine.
Look there's someone surfing and catching the waves
But I'll make sure he's saved for me. Especially for me!
But some people love killing sharks then selling them
in the morning market and seeing how much they weigh
and winning trophies all for nothing,
Soon they will be going, going, gone.

Larisa Williams (10)
Coston Primary School

THE WATERFALL

Slip slop goes
The fish when it's
Falling over the waterfall
Down it drops
Splashing into
The water.
The fish swim away
Very quietly
Slipping behind a big
Rock.

Peter R Seward (11)
Coston Primary School

Rain

Drip drop
Water sounds
Blip blop
Water dripping
Sssh!
Hear it
All clear and bright
I think it's going to go on all night
It's getting calmer
And calmer
And calmer.
It's stopped!

Emman Bhati (10)
Coston Primary School

Sea

Splash, splash
on the sea
Dolphins swimming
free on the
sea.
The dolphins
jumping
flip, flop
Causing a big
drop at the top
like a rainbow.

Thomas Wood (10)
Coston Primary School

BLUE

The look of the sky makes me cry,
Misty moon catches my eye,
Twinkling stars sparkle towards my body,
During the dark night there's nobody.
In the morning in the summery sky
Aeroplanes glide along the fresh looking flowers.
Bluebells move side to side
While the gentle breeze moves left and right.
The blazing sea moves calmly and gently.
My friends' eyes are pretty looking.

Leena Dodhia (10)
Coston Primary School

BLUE

Sky bright up in the early morning,
Midday it starts to snow,
Winds blow the snow into people's gardens.
At night it's cold and windy,
Rubbish rolling around scares you.
The sea splashes against the rocks and makes them slippery and wet,
Some bright doors I go past,
Paper is bright too,
Chalk like the sky.

Gary Johnson (11)
Coston Primary School

Cosmic

Cosmic stars,
Cosmic moon,
Lighting up the sky.

Cosmic lights,
Flickering in the night,
Lighting up the earth.

Cosmic night sky,
Wonderful and bright,
The sight is perfect.

Cosmic planets,
Dark and mysterious,
Spread around the sky.

Cosmic spacecraft,
Spacemen brave and daring,
It is a cosmic world.

Robert Lupton (10)
Collis Primary School

Cosmic

Spaceships, UFO's whizzing by,
Stars shining, glittering
Millions of light years away from earth,
Cosmic planets no one's seen,
Friendly creatures looking out at space,
Evil creatures terrorising a race,
Cosmic Space.

Martyn Davies (11)
Collis Primary School

Cosmic

I stare up into the night sky,
As black as a piece of coal,
Shooting stars whizzing by,
Higher and higher as they go.

Up and up into space,
Floating past the moon,
Shivering and weaving through the night,
Until they've gone, right out of sight.

I look further up into space,
To find lots of planets,
Settled all over the place.

Lorraine Kent (11)
Collis Primary School

Cosmic

I sit and look into
The cosmic skies.

Comets and rockets
Are whizzing by.

Mars and Jupiter are
Far away.

Is anyone on the moon
Today?

Mark Smith (11)
Collis Primary School

Cosmic World

Dark skies, glistening stars,
A gentle touch like a silk sheet.

A heavenly halo surrounds the moon
That shimmers on a peaceful lake.
A shooting star with its burning tail
Is there
But then not.

Over glaciers runs wild the Aurora Borealis.

Towering mountains set off a great avalanche
Rolling and swallowing up anything in its path.

Far away in the hot, gleaming, desert sun
The moving sands slide and glide,
Gigantic shadows cast over canyons.

Great barrier reefs stretch, twist and curl
Through the changing colours of the sea,
That lie still and calm, yet to be seen.

Philip Linter (10)
Collis Primary School

Cosmic

I had a cat called Cosmic,
He was quite a hilarious comic,
He used to look up at the stars,
Indulge in chocolate bars,
And dream he was a red flying comet.

Rachel Ramsay (10)
Collis Primary School

COSMIC

Look up in the sky,
At night,
And you will see
A cosmic sight.

You'll see,
Stars in the sky,
The moon up high
Maybe a star whizzing by.

Once I saw
A comet flying by,
Big and bright,
In the sky.

The moon is,
Like a football.
What would happen
If it were to fall?

B J Pratt (11)
Collis Primary School

COSMIC DANCER

A well known ballerina
Performs in front of lords and Hollywood stars.
(Took a gamble on life - and lost)
She was a bit of a chancer.

Now she performs in front of
Gods and silent stars.
She is now a cosmic dancer.

Emma Hibbert (10)
Collis Primary School

Cosmic

There could be aliens out there,
In the boundless darkness of the galaxy.
In the midst of all the flurry of spaceships
From humans who have now destroyed their planet
And are looking for another source of destruction.

There could be extra-terrestrial life
On planets we have yet to discover
Where human beings have not yet polluted
Or disturbed mother nature who covers the earth in her long,
                                        long flowing gown
But I'm sure they'll find a way.

There could be exotic creatures,
Spying on earth and its evil ways.
Pondering over whether to destroy the strange race
Of beings which walk on two legs,
Who will annihilate the universe some day.

Freddie Ridge (11)
Collis Primary School

Cosmic

The ground shook,
Rumble, rumble, rumble,
Bang, bang, bang,
The spacecraft landed with a thump,
Bump, bump, bump
Came rolling a green man.
Slurp, slurp, slurp.
Thunder and lightning in the sky,
Rain falling from the sky.

Neil Kotecha (10)
Collis Primary School

STARS

Stars, stars, in the sky
Make me happy when I cry,
They shine so bright in the sky,
You often see them fly.

Some stars are small, some are big,
Making patterns in the sky
Just like birds when they fly.

They move across the starlit sky,
Like a twinkle in your eye,
You see them shining in the night
Glowing out towards the light,
Making the earth shine bright.

Scott McKenzie (10)
Collis Primary School

COSMIC

Come, look at this,
Oceans full of fish,
Suns, moons and stars,
Make up this world of ours
If creatures are to survive
Cleaning up will keep them alive.

Thomas Stell (10)
Collis Primary School

COSMIC

The humungus black giant
Loomed over the earth
Stretching for miles and miles
Bigger, longer, wider, immense
Bigger than the earth
So vast I can't imagine it
Blimy, that giant's big!

Phew, I think I'll go back
And think about something a little smaller,
Mmm! how about cosmic dust
It's so small it's *tiny, minuscule.*

That's enough about Cosmic
For now!

Fergus McIntosh (10)
Collis Primary School

COSMIC

Cosmic is a colourful place,
Cosmic is a wonderful place,
The stars of silver,
The moons of gold,
The planets of all colours,
The galaxy looks like glitter,
But all of this,
Comes and consists,
In the colourful,
Wonderful,

    Cosmic.

Lauren Ray (11)
Collis Primary School

COSMIC

Looking up at the sky
Seeing something shining bright
Shimmering in the moonlight,
Up in the night's atmosphere
Flickering down
As if trying to send a message down to us.
The nights become longer
The stars come out for longer
The sky is full of light
From the stars that come out at night.
Looking through my telescope
I spot something different,
It's gone, it's disappeared
Searching, seeking, what was it I saw?
I see the sun coming over the hill,
My day's over,
But maybe next time I'll find it once more.

Kirsty Ivison (11)
Collis Primary School

COSMIC

Cosmic alien astronomers look out for human beings,
Only the shooting stars know if there are human beings out there,
Stars whiz around the planets like bees around a honey pot,
Missions to the galaxy (yum, yum)
It must be hot out there because of the sun,
Cosmic our world is, so please don't damage it.

Jared David Short (11)
Collis Primary School

COSMIC

Space is cosmic,
Calm and peaceful is cosmic,
The sun,
The stars,
The moons,
Mercury, Venus, Earth, Mars, Jupiter
Saturn, Uranus, Neptune, Pluto.
Planets
The stars and moons,
That light up the dark sky at night,
And the sun that shines throughout the day!
A black hole is cosmic,
Silence is cosmic.

Olivia Laura Nixson (10)
Collis Primary School

COSMIC

One day a ship from outer space
Zoomed towards the human race,
It was not big,
It was not small,
Instead it was just mighty tall!

Then a giant almighty
Came from the biggest oil pipe,
The ship buzzed about like an angry bee
And made a crash-landing into the sea.
That was the last I heard of the little men,
I hope they don't come back again!

Gregory Unsworth (11)
Collis Primary School

COSMIC

I've always dreamed of going
into that cosmic world,
Astronauts travel there
so I have been told.

They float around like little balloons,
wandering in space.
Looking on different planets
for some sign of an alien race.

They fly up in rockets,
that go so very fast.
While space probes search on planets
to find out more about their past.

I lie in bed at night
looking at the stars.
I wonder if I'll ever see a supernova
or even land on Mars.

And then I remember Mum's Chocolate Torte
and a smile spreads on my face.
It's way better than anything
I could experience in space.

Samuel Manning (11)
Collis Primary School

Cosmic

I got myself a spaceship,
I flew up to the stars,
I passed the solar system, Jupiter and Mars.

I visited the moon, a big shiny sphere,
My glistening spaceship
Took me on a tour of the universe
To see the planets and their moons.

I saw comets whizzing by
Never stopping for a breath
I came to the edge of the universe,
Finished my trip and went back to earth.

Jemma Holdaway (11)
Collis Primary School

Cosmic

I come from another universe,
I come from far away,
I travelled many galaxies
Until I found your Milky Way.
And now I'm feeling kind of strange,
In a cosmic sort of way.
My spaceship has been vaporised
Into a thousand tiny bits,
So I'm stuck here on this cold, wet earth,
The size of a cosmic pip.

Thomas Caldwell (10)
Collis Primary School

Cosmic!

I was wild and all nature was balanced,
Then came the human race and so began my destruction,
I have withered and am dying,
Testimony to human greed.

I am polluted by machinery and all of mankind,
My rivers now filthy, no more shall wind,
The humans will move to another planet
Leaving me alone to choke on their vomit.

In a swirling mass of darkness and pain,
The putrid air, the acid rain,
Wherever they go,
Let it not happen again.

Cait Orton (10)
Collis Primary School

Cosmic

Cosmic was a cat
A very fat cat
He flew on the moon
And never came back
He sits up there
With his tabby-coloured hair
Happily grinning into space
Everyone thinks it's the man in the moon's face
They don't know it's my fat cat
I just think hey fancy that
That's truly *Cosmic!*

Mungo Coyne (10)
Collis Primary School

COSMIC

Ready to go?
Yep all set.
Gliding, tumbling seeing sights,
We're off to our destination!
The sparkling stars, the whole galaxy,
Is this a dream?
I pinch myself just to make sure,
No, I'm really here!
Another few days to go and we'll be there.
I look down at the earth
It's no bigger than a pea now
Not long now
We'll soon be there!
We're slowing down,
We're here.
I'm being swept off my feet
Oh, hi Gran!

Carla Jane Holding (11)
Collis Primary School

COSMIC!

The night sky is full of stars,
The sun is full of shine.
The moon is like a white globe,
So high above the ground.

The universe is still and peaceful,
The stars and sky still shine,
The cosmic world is shining,
Under the stars and sun.

Victoria Howe (11)
Collis Primary School

Cosmic

Cosmic is the universe
It could go back in reverse.
Then one day it may come around
And then it will fall to the ground.

When the sun comes out in the day,
Everybody goes out to play,
When the sun goes down
It is not the same all around.
Every child has to stay in
That's when it looks grim.
But when you look out of the window at night
You see the stars twinkle like little lights,
You see some shoot across the sky
Which disappear way up high.

Emma Knight (11)
Collis Primary School

Cosmic

Far away in the sky
I saw some elephants floating by
I sent my cosmic rocket up
As there was no gravity I spilt my cup.
I missed the elephants floating past,
So I turned round my rocket and crashed in the grass.

Alex Cox (10)
Collis Primary School

COSMIC

Flying, spinning,
Falling, simmering,
Swirling balls,
Red hot fire,
Up there in that wilderness.

Rings of dust,
Floors of granite.
No gravity allowed.
Life scarce,
Maybe none . . .

Everything is cosmic,
Molecules of rock,
Slabs of ice,
Heat or cold
Boiling or freezing.

Up there in that wilderness,
Planets, comets, boulders,
Out there . . .
In that universe!

Francesca Rose Gray (10)
Collis Primary School

COSMIC

My garden is the cosmos
The land of outer space,
The apple tree my spaceship,
Named The Cosmic kind of grace.

> I'm going to take a trip now,
> Up into the stars,
> I sail towards the garden shed
> Which (of course) is Mars.

SOS please help me,
My fuel tank has burst
I ran into an asteroid
And I'm getting rather fussed.

> Oh dear, oh my, oh me, oh why,
> I'm headed for the moon,
> As you see I really must
> Be getting back quite soon.

Eventually I'm back on earth,
Just in time for tea,
Only then did I remember
I had left behind the key!

Aisha Krupska (10)
Collis Primary School

COSMIC

Cosmic in the sun,
Cosmic in the rain,
Cosmic is the feeling
When I see your face again.

Cosmic in the moon,
Cosmic in the stars,
'Cause cosmic is the emotion
I get when you are near
All emotions, feelings and fear,
All in a single tear.

Cosmic in the sea,
Cosmic on the land.
Cosmic in the sand.

Naomi Kay (10)
Collis Primary School

TIGER, TIGER

Tiger shine so bright,
Shine like the moon and the stars tonight,
The tiger is so bright,
It has orange and black stripes,
I don't like the sound, roaring that roars tonight,
The stormy weather,
Where they will lay tonight.
The forest is as dark as the clouds,
Green is my favourite colour
Where they will shake, shake, shake.

Sarah-Jane Sexton (10)
Deanesfield Primary School

DAYDREAMS

Teachers think I'm writing,
But no, I am playing netball
And scoring all the goals.

Teachers think I'm working,
But no, I'm thinking what I look like,
When I'm older all slim and tall.

Teachers think I'm reading,
But no, I'm thinking about home time,
And what I'm going to do.

Teachers think I'm listening,
But no, I'm thinking about my dad at work,
Fixing broken cars.

Teachers think I'm drawing,
But no, it's my birthday,
I'm eating cakes and playing games.

Teachers think I'm awake and working,
But no, I'm in bed fast asleep,
All warm and cosy!

Rosie Biddlecombe (10)
Deanesfield Primary School

TIGER

A tiger running around so strong and fierce,
Big teeth, eating animals,
But not faster than a cheetah
Beware the tiger is dangerous
Long legs and running in the night.
Blood on the floor and big claws.

Yousef Khalifa (10)
Deanesfield Primary School

HARVEST

Harvest is a time for rabbits
That watch beside country roads,
Dew falls lightly along winding lanes,
Combine harvesters get to work
Cutting the fields of wheat.

Harvest is the cool days
Of the late Indian Summer,
Pheasants darting through the hedgerow,
Tree leaves turning golden.

Harvest is a time
For the smell of hot berry pies,
Purple-mouthed children sit by a blackberry bush,
Thank you Lord, for harvest time.

Thomas Kebble (10)
Deanesfield Primary School

TIGER IN A STORM

There's a tiger in the forest getting soaking wet,
He is looking for prey,
He finds prey, he jumps and catches it.
Now he is happy.
He is hiding from hunters.
Hunters are searching for a tiger in the forest.
The hunters see the tiger and then *bang*
The tiger gets away.

Kurt McKenna (10)
Deanesfield Primary School

DAYDREAMS

It's all quiet in the classroom, my teacher thinks I'm writing,
But she doesn't know what's going through my head,
I think of winning the Jackpot and helping the poor,
Or fighting a dragon until it's dead,
On Wednesdays I think about the netballers,
Whether they are big or small,
I dream about winning the netball tournaments,
Or redecorating my bedroom walls.
Sometimes I dream that I have a car with no roof, and leather seats,
Everybody having the same amount of food and drink,
I dream about a time machine,
That takes me on an adventure,
Then a tap on my shoulder, it's my teacher,
'Oh, sorry Miss!'

Kirsty Treadwell (10)
Deanesfield Primary School

TIGER

Tiger stomping through the jungle
As the wind whizzes through his hair,
The trees waving up above,
It leaps over the tall grass,
While struggling through the stormy wind.

His teeth razor sharp,
His claws could rip you apart,
He could eat your head off.

Jack Hann (10)
Deanesfield Primary School

DAYDREAMS

Mrs Lomax thinks I'm doing maths
Oh no, I'm not!
I'm scoring on my England debut
I also have my own dog
I own all food and drink in the world
I'm helping the poor.

Mrs Lomax thinks I'm reading
But I'm a famous athlete
I also have lots of friends
I have a great car
Wow! an airliner
I'm 150! And I'm in heaven
I wish I had done the land speed record
'David!'
What a dream!

David Newton (11)
Deanesfield Primary School

HARVEST

H   arvest is a time of year when I eat berries,
A   corns are gathered by squirrels
R   oads are full of tractors
V   erity is gathering berries
E   dward is in a big coat.
S   tuart is gathering a marrow.
T   om is in the bush.

Billy Brown (10)
Deanesfield Primary School

DAYDREAMS

Mrs Lomax thinks I'm writing,
But I'm not,
I'm scoring for England
Or winning in the French Open
I'm on a Concorde to America,
Or I'm wrestling in the Royal Rumble,
I'm winning the 400 m in the athletics.

Mrs Lomax thinks I'm reading,
Oh no!
I'm winning the championship powerboat race,
Or winning the lottery,
I'm playing for Man United,
Or I'm making people disappear,
I'm lifting whales with my little finger,
And boxing Frank Bruno,
I'm racing Formula One cars,
Mrs Lomax spots me,
I am in trouble!

Stephen Mooney (10)
Deanesfield Primary School

WALKING ALONE IN THE DARK

I see shadows running and jumping it reminds me of someone coming,
I hear cats, sounding like giant insects,
The trees moving remind me of dark strangers bending over me,
Bushes shaking like long shivering fingers,
I hear footsteps but it is only me,
The moon in the sky like a watch telling me the time,
Clouds shouting down at me telling me what to do.

Tommy Fountain (11)
Deanesfield Primary School

Daydream

I am a famous illustrator,
And everyone knows my name,
I have a Mercedes Benz,
And the wind is rushing through my hair,
Everyone is equal,
And they have all the same.

I've banned all the rubbish,
That people want to buy,
So that people can stay alive,
And not have boring lives.

Suddenly I wake up,
Where has my Mercedes Benz gone?
We're not all equal,
And people haven't stopped buying rubbish
Oh no! I've just been daydreaming.

Matthew Molloy (10)
Deanesfield Primary School

Walking Alone In The Dark

Trees are like big black giants standing in the moonlight,
Stars look like glowing fireflies lighting up the skies,
Bushes are like hairy monsters hiding in the darkness,
Owls sound like ghosts haunting the tree tops,
Clouds look like white fluffy sheep floating in the sky,
The moon is like a watch dangling from the sky.

Lee Harvison (11)
Deanesfield Primary School

HARVEST

Harvest is farmers sweating in the fields,
The dewy webs woven on hedges,
Squirrels gathering food for their long winter's sleep.

Harvest is heavy dark berries on drooping bushes,
The harvest moon glowing in the late evening sky like a fat
                                                    gold watch,
Haystacks like plump sausages lying in the fields.

Harvest is an old church decorated with summer flowers,
Cool perfumed air and cold dark shadows,
Slow tractors chugging down the country lanes.

Aiysha Patel (10)
Deanesfield Primary School

WALKING DOWN THE STREET

Walking down the street reminds me of the zoo,
The motorbikes roar like wild lions,
The cars are honking like crazy monkeys,
The lorries are like elephants parading round the town.

Ambulances run by like leopards in the wild,
Buses are like birds flying to every branch,
The people on bikes are like fish swimming by,
The lamp-posts peer over like tourists watching the animals.

Verity Bristow (10)
Deanesfield Primary School

THE TIGER

His sharp jagged teeth make creatures cower with fear,
As fast as lightning but as silent as a mouse,
His long tail whips out,
The leaves sway in the wind like a boat on a stormy sea.

Hidden by the greenery,
He takes a cautious step forward,
Boom!
The lightning stops the tiger in its tracks.

His fur like fire,
A tree branch snaps,
As the rain begins to fall,
A cowardly zebra runs in fright.

The tiger pounces on the zebra,
And uses its sharp claws to kill it,
It eats it and takes the leftovers to his cubs,
The night is young and the tiger's
Plan has already succeeded.

Thomas Groves (10)
Deanesfield Primary School

GOING ON A SLIDE

The steps are like a ladder from a fire engine going high in the sky,
I am nervous and cold as I wonder, wonder if I will fall down,
When I finally make it to the top I feel like a king from a castle
                                        looking at the world below.
Swooping down like an eagle or sliding down a giraffe's neck.
The poles are like long legs keeping me up.

Ian Smith (11)
Deanesfield Primary School

DAYDREAMS

I have a dream about being a movie star,
Singing and dancing.
I have a dream about having magic powers
So that I can grant anything I wish.
I sometimes think what it would be liké to be an animal
Is it easy or is it hard?
I sometimes think what I should be when I grow up
Should I be a diver,
Looking after fish?
Or should I be a chef,
Making piles and piles of quiche?
I sit and wonder
Looking into thin air
Thinking what I should be when I grow up.

Kelly Tiretis (10)
Deanesfield Primary School

DAYDREAMS

My mum thinks I'm eating my dinner but I'm not
I'm in a Porsche
Driving on the road
I'm living in a grand house
It has a huge swimming pool
I'm on holiday
In Cyprus or America
I've got a little hamster
Running on my lap
I'm on a horse
Galloping through the green fields
I'm daydreaming!

Kelly Eustice (10)
Deanesfield Primary School

My Daydreams

I am at home
Cuddling my dog
Or I'm swimming in a pool of toffee
Drinking it as I go along
I'm James Bond
Protecting all that is good
Maybe I'm on my way to Florida,
On my own first class plane,
Now I am in a Red Arrow
Doing amazing stunts
Or I am sky diving,
I wake up on the floor,
I've fallen off the chair
And everyone is staring at me.

Christopher Marnoch (10)
Deanesfield Primary School

The Tiger

Tiger, tiger shine so bright,
Your marbled eyes glow in the night,
The leaves go crunch,
When he's looking for his lunch,
He looks for his prey,
All the animals hope he won't stay.
The trees bend over,
The thunder roars,
He has his prey,
Now he runs away.

Gemma Warman (10)
Deanesfield Primary School

A Tiger In The Night

The tiger is as fierce as lightning
Big and brave
Watching for his food
Teeth as sharp as a knife
Tiger, tiger in the night,
Orange like a shining sun,
Still hasn't caught his dinner yet,
As the night goes on,
Tiger, tiger in the night,
Watching for his prey.

Hayley Casey (10)
Deanesfield Primary School

Tigers

Black stripes all over his body
Between the stripes it is orange
Having sharp white teeth
No animal is as fierce as a tiger
Hunting in the jungle for his prey
So scared of the rain, thunder and lightning
Do not dare to go near him
He is so fierce
You are risking your own life!

Georgina Lanning (10)
Deanesfield Primary School

TIGER

Now the wind is blowing hard,
Howling and whistling
Like a wild thing.
In the bushes I can see
A lonely tiger staring at me
In his eyes, his glaring eyes,
I see a glowing ball of fire
But behind that I see
That he is frightened just like me.
Lightning lights up the sky
And away he slowly creeps.
Then suddenly he gives a roar,
Then another, and more, and more.
I see his teeth, a brilliant white,
Shining through the stormy night.
I start to run away
Much too afraid to stay.

Lauren Scott (10)
Deanesfield Primary School

THE TIGER

The tiger crawling in the plants
Looking for his den in the night
Fur glistening in the moonlight
Ready to catch his prey
The tiger's tail always sways.

Bradley Gilbert (10)
Deanesfield Primary School

Walking Alone In The Dark

Dark clouds like ghosts looking down at me,
Sounds of trees rattling like a rattlesnake.
A car with no exhaust like a roar of a tiger.
Birds chirping like a mouse that is hovering around me,
Shadows of animals remind me of trees that look at me with
                                          cobwebs all over them.

A spine-chilling thought of trees with fingers pricking at me,
I see an eagle swoop down at me like a big black bat,
Then look at an owl with eyes like a red demon.
The flash from a car light looking at me like a white ghost.
A glow-worm glowing like it's just been frightened by something.

Alex MacDonald (10)
Deanesfield Primary School

The Tiger

A tiger is quick, fast, sneaky as a lion,
The tiger prowls around for its prey like an angry lion,
Its orange fur burns like a raging fire,
Tiger your claws are sharper than the sharpest knife
Suddenly you spot an antelope and you strike,
You eat it, you like it,
And run off to hide,
Tiger runs freely not being hunted.

Charlotte Smith (10)
Deanesfield Primary School

THE YEAR OF THE TIGER

The tiger's eyes are like burning fire,
He leaps and he pounces at each victim.
His bright orange stripes are like the brightest oranges.
He is in the jungle concentrating on his prey,
Nothing can stop him but a vicious hunter,
As he runs through the jungle it is like
The jungle has caught fire from the tiger.
The tiger runs to feed his baby cubs,
This vicious creature prowls around.
He is waiting for another victim to kill.
The black stripes on the tiger are like
An extinguished fire on his back.

Robert Macfarlaine (10)
Deanesfield Primary School

TIGER

Tiger, tiger
Stripes are camouflaged
With trees and plants
His teeth sharper than
Sharks teeth
He creeps upon you
Like a bullet from a gun
He's a motor car in a race.

Anthony Gourlay (10)
Deanesfield Primary School

TIGER

Tiger, tiger of the jungle,
No one dares to make a sound.
Stealthy as the setting in darkness,
As he runs through the jungle.

The crickets start their early morning clicking,
While he lies as motionless,
As death waiting,
To pounce on an unsuspecting prey.

Daniel O'Brien (10)
Deanesfield Primary School

THE TIGER

The tiger is a very fierce animal,
The tiger is a very dangerous animal
Teeth as sharp as a blade
Orange skinned coat
With black thick lines.
The cheetah is the tiger's best friend
The tiger's tail is a whip
His eyes are like marbles
Shining in the night.

Dawn Wood (10)
Deanesfield Primary School

TIGER IN THE BUSH

The jungle is noisy,
Animal's scared,
Apart from one,
That is the tiger,
Black and orange,
Very sharp teeth,
With a wet nose,
Very sharp claws,
Very strong,
And very fierce,
His roar as loud as thunder.

James McMillan (10)
Deanesfield Primary School

WALKING ALONE IN THE DARK

Owls hooting with bright yellow eyes that remind me of a shiny torch,
Leaves rustling as the wind blows them across the ground like
people running.
Trees swaying like witches grabbing you with their knobbly fingers,
Bats squeaking remind me of when the witches laugh spookily,
I think I hear footsteps coming closer behind me,
Wolves howling showing their razor sharp teeth,
I hear a noise in the distance, it sounds like a ghost but it's just
the owls hooting.

Hayley Greaves (10)
Deanesfield Primary School

TIGER

The night is dark.
The world is asleep,
all except the king.
Everywhere silent but,
like a motorbike my heart,
increases its speed and *rrooaarr*
the tiger sees me.
I run and luckily I get away,
but he has not given up yet.
He goes to look for his prey
and the jungle is quiet and then
suddenly I hear a cry and a roar
the tiger is once again happy.

Katie-Jane Sams (10)
Deanesfield Primary School

THE TIGER

The tiger in the jungle at night,
his tail swishes from left to right.
With lightning flashing,
and colours clashing
the jungle stands strong and tall.
All that moves is the waterfall.
The birds are flying
to warmer climates,
but in the morning all is normal.

Erhyn Wingrove-Owens (10)
Deanesfield Primary School

ALONE IN THE DARK

The dark trees like ghostly people stretching their
                                arms out to get me,
The moon's glow covers me as he smiles,
Shadows coming towards me like dark creatures from
                                    out of space,
The wind whistling as it twists and twirls around me,
Newspapers rustling somewhere in the gloom,
The hooting owl's eyes glow in the night darkness.

Zoê Cornish (10)
Deanesfield Primary School

WALKING IN THE DARK

The owl's eyes are staring and his voice is hooting,
I can see shadows slowly moving with the wind,
Even the tall dark trees look like they are following me.
A car goes by, it sounds like a lion roaring for food,
Low down bushes feel like prickling fingernails on my legs,
Leaves rustle, I think there's someone behind me,
Owls hooting like ghosts, calling to each other.
Now I am out of the dark, safe from everything.

Stacey Beard (11)
Deanesfield Primary School

A Street Of Noisy Traffic

There is a whole big road full of noisy traffic.
There's a huge red bus which roars like a lion.
A bicycle is like a small creature coming towards me.
The lampposts are like tall, thin fingers looking over the road.
The cars are swishing down the busy road like a flash of lightning.
As I go to cross the road all the vehicles stop like a sudden crash of
thunder.

James Lanning (11)
Deanesfield Primary School

Tiger

Tiger, tiger
Waiting for his prey.
Tiger, tiger
Fierce as can be.
Tiger, tiger
Sneaking through the grass.
Tiger, tiger
Don't go near.
Tiger, tiger
Roaring in the night.

Louise Clarke (10)
Deanesfield Primary School

Cosmic World

The stars are out there small and bright,
But the sun gives out most of the light,
Then suddenly a rocket shoots up to the sky,
And I knew it was going to be bye, bye.

And from the rocket I saw the Milky Way,
There were aliens moulding their clay,
The truth is out there said Mulder and Scully,
When I go to school I'm sure kids will bully.

We landed on the moon, craters all around,
If I took a photo I'm sure I'd get a pound,
Then someone came up to me there was a big boom,
I thought it was going to take me to my doom.
The cosmic world is a weird place!

Nisha Shah (12)
Elmgrove Middle School

The Moon

I wish I was Neil Armstrong going to the moon.

Oh no, I've just seen an alien,
Quick - hide behind the rocket.
It's OK now, it's gone
It was an alien with four eyes, fourteen legs and six arms.

We are going on the rocket home
Quick swerve it's a meteorite.
It's coming to the rocket
We are going to our doom . . .

Nicola Bubenzer (11)
Elmgrove Middle School

THE COSMIC POEM

Cosmic is a funny world,
With planets that twirl and twirl
With the Milky Way
The aliens see it every day.
High up in space,
You'll see their face,
Yellow and green,
Nasty and mean
Or are they kind
And have nothing on their mind?
I have to stop writing this poem
For there is a meteorite coming
Quick! Hide under the chair
Life is so unfair.

Bijal Savadia (12)
Elmgrove Middle School

The Martians and Me

Wouldn't you love to come face to face
With an alien from outer space
They have four eyes
      eight fingers
      and two legs
They see every move we make
And every step we take

There they were right in front of me
I asked them where they came from
They told me they lived on Mars
They took me into space
And showed me all the stars

I was in space
What a wonderful place
      the stars filled the skies
      and dazzled my eyes

Was it a dream
Was it all real
I don't know
But I know who will.

Natasha Kwaskowska (12)
Elmgrove Middle School

MISSION POSSIBLE

Quake was getting worried as he could see the
Spaceship about to enter earth.
They hit the earth.
Quake and the MIB were ready.
They started to shoot, so I gave them the boot.
The missiles were ready and Quake came out all steady.
They took off rapidly.
We dodged out of the way as the shooting star brushed past us,
It was dark then I heard a bark,
We landed on Mars and it was very cold
Six aliens came out and started to shout,
Will Smith got his gun, and had some fun.
Galaxy Defended!

Kishan Joshi (12)
Elmgrove Middle School

BEGINNINGS

Slowly beginning with wings and eyes
Flying with another bird
Singing and dancing in the sky
In the dark or in the light
Singing with joy and laughter.

In the trees on the floor
Singing sweetly singing any day, anywhere
They're still singing with joy
They slowly begin to sweetly sing
On the earth (afar?)

Rebecca Singer (11)
Frithwood Primary School

THREE WEIRD BEASTS

The Big-Headed Bingaling Bomabong,
Sat in the mountains and roared out a song.
A snake crawled right up, and ate up his pup,
And he brought down his head on a gong.

The Wikkywok Willowan Wakkywiv ,
Sat on the seashore and looked like a skiv.
He waved his umbrella, which whirred like a propeller,
And he is never seen without with.

The Fat Povelpapperatpover,
Nibbled a four-leafed clover.
It gave him good luck, and turned into one buck,
And he ran off with a lady from Dover.

Peter Shelton (10)
Frithwood Primary School

AUTUMN IS HERE

A   utumn is here
U   nder the oak tree
T   here are acorns
U   sually warm, now it's cold
M   ore leaves on the ground
N   ow the leaves change colour
S   o autumn is here.

H   appy days
E   very day
R   ed and yellow leaves
E   verywhere on the ground.

Jack Bennington (10)
Frithwood Primary School

Sunday Morning Football

Football's today, I'm determined to win,
If we do then I will surely grin,
I'm in goal, I hope I don't let any in,
Come on our strikers,
Get a few in!

My boots are clean,
And I am so keen,
Here comes the opposition's striker,
Gosh he looks mean!

The crowd is shouting,
The fans are cheering the other side to win,
My manager looks worried,
I think he needs a gin!

Here comes that mean striker,
Dribbling the ball,
He's taken a great shot
Gosh that was hot!

I went in brave,
But it was not to be a save
The ball hit me in the face,
And nearly put me in my grave!

Another loose,
But that's okay
Because whatever happens
I still love playing football any way!

Antony Bronson (10)
Frithwood Primary School

BONFIRE NIGHT

Bonfire night
The fire's are alight
They are blazing in the night
Rockets being lit
Exploding in the sky
They are going to split.
One big rocket
Went *capow!*
Everyone said, 'Wow!'
Firemen came and put
The fire out.
Everyone started to shout,
That's the end of bonfires, what a fright
It was the end of a great night.

Andrew Sinclair (11)
Frithwood Primary School

MY PET

My pet is small but naughty,
What is my pet?
My pet has a ball, house and wheel,
What is my pet?
My pet has a cage and nibbles a lot,
What is my pet?
My pet is also sneaky and fast,
My pet is a hamster!

Alfie Mancini (10)
Frithwood Primary School

ONCE IN A BLUE MOON

It has been a long day for the sun
As it slowly falls asleep
It gets darker
As the moon awakes
The stars come out
While the moon turns blue
And the owls start to *twit twoo!*

Also the bats awake along with the foxes and rats
They scuffle along the woodland floor,
And in and out of the big tree door
Admiring the lovely silent blue moon
Finally the moon drifts asleep
As the sun awakes and watches over the world.

Pagan Leigh Toland (11)
Frithwood Primary School

ANIMALS

Animals, animals,
Different kinds of animals
Dogs, cats, rats and bats
Different kinds of animals,
Rabbits, mice, hamsters, two guinea pigs
Different kinds of animals
Different wild animals, pet animals
Different kinds of animals.

Lianne Winter (10)
Frithwood Primary School

MY FAMILY

I have a brother called Joe,
His biceps he likes to show,
To all the girls on the go,
Oh I have a brother called Joe.

I have a gran called Flo,
She likes to be called Po,
Oh no - what a name, it is so insane!
Oh I have a gran called Flo.

I have a mum called Sue,
Oh dear - she's as wet as dew,
She is so plain and plants grain,
Oh I have a mum called Sue.

I have a dad called Brad,
Oh he is a big cuddly mad dad,
He's allergic to cats and hates my plaits,
Oh I have a dad called Brad.

So I have a family,
Who's surname is Makree,
We chew on gum and have lots of fun,
Oh I have a family.

Louisa Willoughby (11)
Frithwood Primary School

SEASIDE

I started the day playing on the sand,
Listening to the music of the band.

The gentle sound of the waves,
Going in and out of the caves.

We went out in a boat,
I had to wear my waterproof coat.

The boat started to rock to and fro
The man beside me started to row.

We jumped off the boat up some stairs
We went past some trotting mares.

We got in the car,
And drove to a bar,
Which was our house?
I accidentally stepped on a woodlouse,
Eventually we found our house.

Alice Whalley (10)
Frithwood Primary School

MY DAD'S JOB

When I grow up I would like to be one of these:
A policemen, a fireman, or a Grand Prix motor driver
I would even like to be in the Royal Air Force
But most of all I would like to be like my dad
A milkman!

Jonathan Parker (10)
Frithwood Primary School

Molly

The RSPCA we went to, to get a little moggy,
We found the purr-fect pet and we called her Molly.
It was the beginning of a friendship between a girl and cat,
And from that day forwards, it's been just like that.
I love my little Molly, she's my feline friend at home,
I love my little Molly, but I hate it when she moans.

Rachael Steele (11)
Frithwood Primary School

Rivers

R ushing rivers everywhere.
I n the mountains they may flow.
V ery, very fast they go, speeding past,
E very sound is music to my ears
R oaring water, baby fish swimming past
S ome are swimming past very fast.

Cassy O'Neill (10)
Frithwood Primary School

Winter

W hite snowflakes flutter down,
I t does not make a sound,
N ice in the house cuddled up warm,
T he children and the adults snuggle up tight,
E vening comes, the children fall asleep,
R ed reindeers' noses in the air, magic is everywhere.

Amira Tejani (10)
Frithwood Primary School

THE GARDEN

The garden is where the creepy crawlies lurk
The spider is the one I dread the most,
And woodlouse is the one I like to toast.
The garden is where the creepy crawlies lurk
The butterfly is the prettiest
And the fly is the ugliest
The garden is where the creepy crawlies lurk,
Spiders, butterflies and ladybirds too,
They're in your garden too.
So watch out!

Shruti Patel (10)
Frithwood Primary School

A RABBIT POEM

You twitch your nose when you smell,
You jump about when you're held
You love to run in the run outside
You jump up and down filled with pride.
You eat your hay as slow as can be,
You eat your food with glee.
After you've had a slurp of your drink
You jump to one side to think.
Then you hop as fast as can be
To come along and play with me,
And when the day has been done
I bring you in from the run
I place you in your cosy hutch,
Turn out the light, rabbit good night.

Alison Powell (10)
George Spicer Primary School

Florida

My amazing trip to Florida
Led me to many adventures.
First we went to Sea World
Magic Kingdom and Typhoon Lagoon.
Then we went to Universal Studios
That really was so cool,
But I wasn't brave enough,
To go on the biggest ride of all.
The apartment that we stayed in,
Really was so good,
Plus the view from the balcony
Was way better than the film Robin Hood!
My amazing trip to Florida,
Really was so great,
And I would never swap it,
For anything that I've ever ate!
My memories of Florida,
Hold everlasting joy,
I would love to go,
With all my family,
For then they would see why.

Melissa Ann Brown (10)
George Spicer Primary School

My Poem

My box is made of motorbike stunts
fast Ferrari's and a
trip to the USA

It's as big as a truck
and shaped like a pyramid and
this is how it opens. All the
sides except the bottom disappear!

My most precious memory
In the box
Is when I first got my bike and
on a cold spooky night
I rode it around then
crashed on the ground and found I
fell out my bed.

Then I was
attacked
by a colossal catastrophic catastrophe
cat from Canada!

Daniel Chapman (10)
George Spicer Primary School

The Night Sky

The night sky is filled with stars
I can just about see tiny Mars
The moon is glimmering in the sky
I wonder how it stays up so high
I wonder what it's really like out there
But all I can do is just stare and stare.

Allison Edwards (10)
George Spicer Primary School

HOLIDAY NIGHTMARE

Last year's camping holiday,
Was not exactly fun,
It rained and snowed the whole week through
With not a sign of sun.

Then brother Michael wet the bed,
And little Anne was sick,
Sister Carol moaned and grumped,
Not to mention Mick!

Dad was really in a mood,
Because the tent was torn,
He screamed and swore the whole day through
Right until next morn.

Yes, last year's camping holiday,
Was not that fun at all,
Mum and me were on our own,
Until she broke the stool!

Catherine Bradly (10)
George Spicer Primary School

MY MOTHER

Rubies are rare Emeralds are too
But they aren't as rare as a mother like you.
You have long blonde hair that sparkles like gold
You have big blue eyes that sparkle in the moonlight
But now she thinks she's like a granny
But we always say not to worry,
Just make yourself a nice hot curry.

Ashley Louise Wright (10)
George Spicer Primary School

THE GARDEN

Christmas is over and winter's end is near,
This is our favourite time of the year.
Time to plant our flowers and cut the weeds,
We have to attend to our garden's needs.
Dad spends all the time in the vegetable plot,
Tomatoes, lettuce, carrots, beans, we've got the lot.
A little water, a little sun,
The flowers will blossom and the birds will come.
It's a lovely sight to see,
Butterflies, birds, flowers and bees,
Some flowers grow old no more colours,
Some flowers keep their colours longer than others.
Dad will soon cut everything down,
But still, not to worry, life goes on underground.

Joanna Costa (10)
George Spicer Primary School

MY POEM

There's a box in my head made of flowers, friends and my dog Katie,
My box is bigger than my mum and dad put together,
My box will one day burst open like a cracker,
Inside my box is my family,
In my box is a memory about when I got my hamster called Poppy,
In my box is a memory about the last time I held my rabbit called
                                                                                             Bungie,
Inside my box is a mushy muddy pie from Mexico.

Tom Hall (10)
George Spicer Primary School

PETS

I am a puppy
Playfully, playing
In the field
By the dairy.

I am a kitten
Fighting and wrestling
Nice and cosy
In my basket.

I am a rabbit
All furry and fluffy
Twitching, itching
My feet are rough.

I am a parrot
I am a cool dude
I can say lots of words
But some of them are rude.

I am a fish
Swimming round and round
I would like to be a silver fish
But now I am round.

Holly Kalogirou (10)
George Spicer Primary School

SHADOWS BEHIND ME

Shadows behind me what shall I do
Hiding behind a tree
A bit hungry I'm still scared
Don't know it could be a *ghost*
Or maybe something else
What shall I do?
I'm scared
Big shadows getting bigger by the minute
Everybody's in their house
I did not succeed
Nobody will believe what I've seen
Drying my feet from the rain
My mum is going mad I can hear her shouting
Everybody is hoping for me.

Samantha Rayner (10)
George Spicer Primary School

PUPPIES

Puppies are cute and sweet
They like to run, sleep and eat,
They run around being mad all day,
They love a fuss and like to play.
My puppy Spotty
Is all dotty
And now we call him Spot.
He loves me and I love him
And he loves sleeping in my sister's cot.
My puppy is sometimes sad
But really he's not that bad!

Kirsty Lipscombe (10)
Harmondsworth Primary School

THE BODY

My ear hears everything
Even the silliest little things
My ear hears everything
Even things that go ping
My ear hears everything
Especially the church bell
That goes ding, dong, ding.

My mouth moves like the wind,
My mouth stretches and bends
Moves and curls
Like the wind that swirls
My mouth moves like the wind.

My mouth, my ears,
My arms, my limbs
All move like the wind.

Rachel Dent (10)
Harmondsworth Primary School

SPRING

See the blossom on the trees,
Listen to the humming bees,
The seeds are popping into flowers,
Hopefully no more little showers,
Daffodils yellow,
Yes spring is here,
The little baby lambs appear.
Little rabbits leaping around,
Just think of that lovely spring sound.

Victoria Simmonds (10)
Harmondsworth Primary School

I Remember, I Remember

I remember, I remember
The house where I was born,
The little window where the sun
Came peeping in at morn.

I remember, I remember
The roses red and white
The violets and the lily cups,
Those flowers made of light!

I remember, I remember
The fir trees dark and high
I used to think their big tall tops
Were close against the sky.

Sophie Price (10)
Harmondsworth Primary School

Ocean Sea

I look at the ocean sea roaring
towards me I feel the ocean
breeze falling down on to my
body the waves come rolling
right beyond the wet soggy sand I watch the children
playing beach ball games
leaving me out then a salt
tear comes leaking from my eye
falls on to the sand and dries
away and the palm trees wave
their leaves trying to give an extra breeze.

Charlotte Connolly (11)
Hythe School

THE BIG DAY

I was the shooter standing by
Had to catch the netball,
Try, try, try!
Shoot, shoot! Everybody said,
But I tried a quick pass back instead.

Then I got the ball,
I looked at the net,
My hands were frozen,
My feet were set.
It's a goal! It's a goal,
Hooray! Hooray!
The netball match
A brilliant day.

Sharon Appleton (10)
Hythe School

HAVING FUN

Me and my friend drive my sister round the bend
Doing stuff we shouldn't
Running around
Playing around
Doing what we can.
When it's time for bed, we run like the shot of a gun
Dodging and diving from my sister
Oh, we have so much fun.
Me and my friend drive my sister round the bend.

Goal keeping is fun too.
Dodging and diving to stop the ball hitting the back of the net.
When a striker comes one on one, I close my eyes and run
Running off my line and back again catching the ball.
When the ref gives a penalty
Oh what a feeling to save them!
Oh what a feeling to play in the premiership!
All the top names like Chelsea and Manchester United
Oh goal keeping is fun.

Jason Townsend (11)
Hythe School

LITTLE RONNIE

I bet he has lips as red as a rose
A little round button nose
Cheeks as soft as a peach
Hair as soft as a bowl of flour
Eyes as blue as the ocean sea
Eyelashes as long as can be
Hair as blond as the sun in the sky
A baby
As you walk into his room
There is a smell that fills the air
A smell of baby powder and soft curly hair
A mobile with little boats on
Every twinkle tells a song
Every cupboard, every drawer
Tells a picture or something more
Every window has a sunset
Every teddy has a smile
Go on have a look
It's all worth your while.

Stacey Lynn Hill (11)
Hythe School

BABY SOPHIE

Her eyes as blue as the ocean,
Lips as red as a rose and a little button nose
Her cry like a dolphin,
Her hair as blonde as sand going along in
Her pushchair holding her mummy's hand
But now the bath time has come so she'll
Throw the soap on the floor.
Then she'll sleep and think of the things
She has done and tomorrow she'll think of some more.

Katie Anne Harding (10)
Hythe School

IF I WAS A FLY

If I was a fly on the window,
If I was a fly on the wall.
I would listen to what people say,
And they wouldn't know I was there at all
I would listen to their dreams and hopes
I would listen to stories of fishes.

Stephanie Dowsett (10)
Hythe School

The Swan

The swan swimming in the river.
A neck like a giraffe
A beak like a nutcracker
Eyes like the stars
Feet like twigs snapping
Sparkling wings sparkling in the sunlight
Flying all night and day
Tired, hungry and thirsty
A feathered coat like the snow
That's the swan.

Lee Garland (11)
Hythe School

My First Step

I was feeling brave
I tried to stand
I shook myself
I stepped forward
I'd finally walked
I don't know how but I had
I'd finally walked
But then my dream ended
I fell over and I cried.

Thomas James Flanagan (11)
Hythe School

THE RAINFOREST

I am a venus fly trap
I'm here to collect flies.
I'm buried in between ferns.
I'm completely out of sight.
It's humid and the ground is soggy.
Trees all different shapes and sizes.
The rainforest ground damp and moist
Caused by the down pours of rain.
The smell of damp wood is, yuck.
But the tweets from the birds lift my spirits up.
My heart is filled with happiness.
Some noises are not too nice,
Like the sound of the chain saws
Cutting into the tree trunks
Snakes slither round my stem tickling
As they make way.
It's dark and dingy, just nice for me.
Some flowers glisten and dazzle with their beautiful colours.
Tree frogs perched on tree trunks and branches.
It's noisy day and night.
No peace at all.
Now I hope that you can see
That the rainforest has its nature
Please don't destroy it.
It's not fair.
Animals and plants need their rightful habitats to survive.

Michelle Condon (10)
Hayes Park Primary School

WHY ME

I don't want to go to school today,
As I know what will happen.
The same thing that happened yesterday,
And the day before that.
I know as I turn the corner I'll hear the same
chants and everything I prayed that wouldn't
happen does.
The same group of five shouting the same things.
Tipping up my bag and ripping work and books.
They tell me that my shoes are old and stupid,
They pull my hair and kick me.
And I think, *Why? Why me? What have I done?*
When will this torture end?
I dare not tell anyone as they said they would
make my life a living hell.
I cry myself to sleep and pray that they would find
someone else to pick on.
Then as I open the door I kiss my mum good bye
I take a few steps outside I'm like a cautious baby
taking its first steps.
Inside I tremble I slowly gather a little more
courage and steadily walk a little faster.
Then as I turn the corner my blood turns into
Burning, boiling, bubbling water
And I think
Why me?

Lauren Coyle (11)
Hayes Park Primary School

THE SPACE RACE

It's time for space race 21
The last space race was in 1900
It was the 20th space race
Unfortunately for Pluto the scores have remained the same
ever since God made the world.

Now let's meet our racers,
We have the 'all mighty *Mercury*'
He is the fastest of the lot,
He has won every race since they started racing,
He is now going for lucky race 21.
Next we have *Venus*
He has come 2nd in every race.
Now we have all been waiting to see most colourful and
favourite planet of all
It is planet *Earth*.
The other racers are,
Mars, Jupiter, Saturn, Uranus, Neptune and slow old Pluto.
Our racers have to race around the *Sun* to claim their order of position.

It's race time now in the Galaxy
And they're off
In the lead there is *Mercury and then Venus, Earth, Mars,*
Jupiter, Saturn, Uranus, Neptune and Pluto.
The race has now ended,
The order remained the same all the way through the race and for
the last 20 races.
To find out who wins you have to wait another 100 years to find out.
This is *Amandeep Shihn (age 10)* reporting the *Space Race.*

Amandeep Shihn (10)
Hayes Park Primary School

EXAMS

I sit there my brain hurting,
The teacher giving out the sheets,
I look at my sheet,
I look at the questions,
The teacher tells us we can start,
I look again at the questions
I wish I knew the answers,
My brain starts hurting again,
I put my pen down on the paper and write
I knew it was wrong,
I rub it out,
Now it looks a mess,
I look around they are all writing,
I wish I wasn't me.

Jenni Bull (10)
Hayes Park Primary School

THE BARN

I hear the beams creaking loudly.
I see the cobwebs clinging.
I hear the wild wind whistling and waving.
Like the sound of someone snoring.
I feel the cosy warm straw.
I hear the rain that pours.
I see the twinkle of light.
But still, it does not make the barn bright.
The floor is a carpet of dust.
All the metal is covered with rust.
There's a tatty and creaky old door.
And the sound of that wind really roars.

Jessica Brooks (10)
Lady Bankes Junior School

THE BARN

When a foot lays on the floor,
It's like a creaky floorboard,
About to snap.
Cobwebs tickle on your face,
And the dust on your shoes.
Holes on the roof,
Holes on the floor,
The massive pile of straw to your side.
Spiders and creatures crawling about.
The swinging lantern blinking,
On and off,
On and off,
Trip over the stones without sight,
Hear the noisy creaky door,
Smacking against the wooden walls.

Jack Lisi (10)
Lady Bankes Junior School

RAILWAY PATTERY

Speeding along like a herd of hyenas,
Just like a rocket charging to Venus.
Green bulging bushes prickling past,
Big brick houses going fast.
Racing like a bird in the sky,
Parks full of swings, swinging high.
Other stations whizzing by,
With a glimpse from my eye.

Jamie Campbell (10)
Lady Bankes Junior School

Railway Poetry

I am sitting on a train bored stiff,
Look out the window,
There's my cousin Biff.
Whizzing along as if we're in a battle field,
I'm glad I'm not the one holding that shield.
I know we're in Metro-Land,
It seems like we're in Disneyland.
There is a cockerel calling,
There are lots of people falling.
At last we're in the open air,
With lots of animals to care.
We're going through a field
With lots of horse and cattle,
It seems to me like we're in Seattle.
It's time to say bye for we are home,
But first we must get an ice-cream cone.

Katrina Zimmerman (10)
Lady Bankes Junior School

Locomotive

The locomotive lashes down the track
Through tunnels and over bridges
A stampede stamping, swirling round corners
A tornado tearing through the countryside
Wrecking the view, whipping up the plants, trees and flowers
Hurrying spiders scurrying into the tunnel to save their silk web
But the twister's here again
Blowing it away into the distance
Back into the countryside.

Lois Beaven (10)
Lady Bankes Junior School

The Barn

The spooky creaky floors squeak in the barn,
The grey tiny mice scatter around the barn,
The flickering white candles glow bright and luminous,
The tall brown trees shiver in the wind,
The juicy colourful berries cling to the branches,
The yellow sparkling lantern swings in the wind,
The blue fresh raindrops trickle through the holes,
The pile of cold rusty straw sways from side to side,
The snowflakes shaped cobwebs shine like the sun,
The crunchy crispy leaves disappear in the mist,
Never to be seen again,
Never to be seen again . . .

Bradley Thomas (10)
Lady Bankes Junior School

The Barn

The lantern swings from side to side
With the rain spitting through the holes
The roof
The cracks
The flame manages to stay alight
With the wind howling
Throwing the barn door open
The hay and straw blows away
I turn to see cobwebs
Cobwebs everywhere
The lantern starts to fade
To fade, to fade . . .

Matthew West (10)
Lady Bankes Junior School

THE BARN

Outside the wind is weeping,
While inside some children shelter,
Hiding and huddling,
From outside's new death.
Terrified of what will happen next.
The barn is barb wire to them,
Saving them from the plague.
Candle giving them waxy light,
Bread, fruit and vegetables giving them healthy food,
Stone giving them a smooth table,
Straw giving them a comfortable bed.
Outside is very different,
No longer smelling of sweet summer roses,
The smell of death in the airy air,
Death swinging from house to house.
For years it carries on,
Until a fire strikes,
Leaving them with nothing,
But gone the plague.

Laura Zimmerman (10)
Lady Bankes Junior School

UNIVERSE

The dashing moonlight dodging through the miniature stars,
Going on a smooth journey all around the dark space,
A screaming alarm clock awakening the bright sun,
Planets spinning, getting dizzier moment by moment,
All planets melting like
Butter in a saucepan.

Joe Perry (10)
Lady Bankes Junior School

THE SOLAR SYSTEM

Mercury
Mercury is a burning ball standing beside the sun,
It is a blue spot in a dark mouth,
Twirling like a ball across the ground.

Venus
Venus is a hot ball standing between Mercury and Earth,
The yellow and black spot shining in a dark room.

Earth
Earth is a rotten apple,
It is a tennis ball in the skies,
It has frosted blue water scattered around it.

Mars
Mars is a lump of red dust,
It is a dot with two dots beside it.

Jupiter
Jupiter is like melted marshmallows,
Red chocolate, caramel and mustard

Saturn
Saturn is like an orange with mustard dripping,
It has a bigger circle around it.

Uranus
Uranus is a cold ball of ice forming a ball.

Neptune
Neptune is a snowball thrown in the air.

Pluto
Pluto is like frosty ice glittering with orange juice and melted marshmallows.

Epu Choudhury (10)
Lady Bankes Junior School

The Barn

It's cold and dark outside, colder than can be,
The wind is howling and the tree is waving over to me.
The barn we go in for winter is very nice and warm,
We will stay in there till next spring's summery dawn,
With barley, hay and straw,
and lots, lots more.
The beams are creaky,
Floorboards squeaky,
Food and veg everywhere,
There even maybe a little scare!
We are so excited,
We won't be in the dark,
We will have candles,
But outside the wind is fierce like a shark.
We will sleep in the straw for our beds,
Where we will lay our sleepy heads!

Kate Louise Balkin (10)
Lady Bankes Junior School

Locomotive

Speeding along as fast as a cheetah
Whizzing along scraping against the bushes
It's so fast, I think it is an Inter-City
As fast as a galloping horse racing along
Going as fast as a bird in the sky
Flicking by just like lightning
We're slowing down now, this is my stop
Off the train, now to the shop.

Stephanie Alam (10)
Lady Bankes Junior School

THE BARN!

The place is gloomy, dark and spooky,
It's got hay on the floor as well as mud,
It's all taken place in a creepy barn,
A spooky barn,
A messy barn,
I felt cold, very cold,
It looks familiar,
I had to use a bright finger for my light,
The month was September,
It was raining a downpour,
The wind was gushing past me,
Like horses racing past me,
I had to get up here,
Because of the plague,
Now it's my home,
And I'm all alone.

Eileen Chapman (10)
Lady Bankes Junior School

THE BARN

In the hay the rats lay.
Sleeping in the warm.
As the day is now dawning.
The rats light their eyes up.
As they stare and wonder.
They start to run.
But then they stop.
They go and hide in the hay.
As four people enter the room.

Lisa-Marie (10)
Lady Bankes Junior School

THE BARN

The barn has a sweet side to it,
With the blowing of the trees,
Howling like wolves.
The river trickles through the woods,
Into the lonely, misty village,
The plague village.
The sun squeezes through tatty, rusty cracks,
Into the old wooden barn,
Where the honey coloured hay shines,
On their happy faces as they lay there.
The hill stoops lower than a stooped spoon.
A log matching the colour of the barn,
Rolls from side to side.
But then there's a bad side to it,
With the cobwebs whiter than can be.
The corners darken each day,
As the mice hide,
Their yellowish cheese away.

Chris Simmonds (10)
Lady Bankes Junior School

THE NIGHT SKY

The sun is a bright red tomato
bursting out with scorching flames
and with its rays it shines upon
the dirty, dusty lanes.
As the sunset begins it turns the sky golden red,
then the moon casts its silvery glow
in the sky above your head.

Jennifer Hanrahan (10)
Lady Bankes Junior School

COSMIC

Around the earth we travel,
In a spacecraft,
Discovering the beauties of the living planet,
The most remarkable machines are created on it,
The only planet with water and land,
For humans, animals and creatures to survive on,
Around the earth we travel.
In a hot air balloon,
Breathing the pure fresh air,
Flying high, high above the eagle's tomb,
Finding strange animals in the secret forests,
Learning ways the animals live.
Around the earth we travel,
In a jet aeroplane,
Landing into different worlds,
Meeting other people,
Understanding their ways of life,
Enjoying our period of time with another group of friends.
Around the earth we travel,
In a motor racing car,
Speeding away past other motorists,
Letting the wind fly past our faces,
Riding along with a family of friends,
To a theme park to have great fun.
Around the earth we travel,
By walking,
Passing other pedestrians,
Meeting friends and neighbours,
Greeting them along our path,
Soon we say goodbye to them, to meeting them again, next time.

Rabiah Chaudhry (11)
Islamia Primary School

I CAN FLY

I can fly
High in the sky
Where the birds are far up
Touching the clouds
Hearing the sound of the wind.
Space is near
A dragon is here
Breathing his hot breath down my neck!
I'm in fear
Now comes the fire
As it hits I awake
In a cold sweat.
It was a nightmare
I take a sigh of relief
And go back to sleep.

Paul Mant (12)
Longfield Middle School

OBSESSION

You are the one in my heart makes the flames of hope
burn higher,
The one who with one touch can heal my broken heart,
The one whose eyes show so much love and affection,
You are the one who doesn't just say 'I care,'
But shows it.
You, whose smile brightens up my day,
And whose voice speaks soft and tender words which
Soothes my soul,
You, who till the day my soul flies with the birds,
I shall love forever and ever and ever.

Mitin Dattani (12)
Longfield Middle School

DREAM

Sometimes I dream about things I have seen,
Or things I have said, heard or done!
But from where come the dreams that make you scream
That fill you with terror, hatred and error
Or sadness, darkness?
Who makes the dream that makes you feel sad?

Who makes the dream about the other side?
Where you feel safe
And you don't need to hide?

Who makes the dream
Where you see someone who has passed
To tell you their friendship
Will always last?

Who makes the dream?
Yes, who makes the dream?
We will never know.
But I'm glad we have dreams.
It cleans our thoughts, sad and happy,
Relives memories of loved ones who've passed.

I hope dreams last.

Ashley Strawbridge (11)
Longfield Middle School

Birth

I am in my mother's womb,
Warm and serene.
Effortlessly getting everything I need,
Water . . . food.
It will soon be time to start a new life
In a new place
New experiences.

I am now in this strange place called Earth.
My mum sits smiling at me lovingly.
I am so close to her
I feel the warmth of her breath on my face.
Somebody walks in.
He is called Dad.
He is happy to see me,
Well I think he is but now he is crying!
What have I done to make you cry?
Have I brought you sadness?
No, he is overwhelmed
And that is the feeling of love.

Katie Leahey (12)
Longfield Middle School

My Cat

My cat is as black as soot
He purrs like a helicopter
His whiskers are like black straw
His eyes are as green as grass
His nose is as red as a rose
I love my cat.

Clare Molloy (10)
Lavender Primary School

AUTUMN ORCHARD

Autumn leaves,
Orchard trees,
Ripe apples falling, the -
Lazy wasps adoring.
Hedgehogs rustling,
Birds gathering,
Squirrels collecting, hiding, hoarding,
Wind's blowing fast at me,
Sun setting in the sky,
Bright orange caught my eye,
Time for the nest,
My orchard's at rest.

Nikki Webb (10)
Lavender Primary School

THE HIDDEN BUD!

Nothing's happened,
What's going on?
First it was open,
But now it's gone.
Mum opened the curtains,
It opened its arms.
Nightfall came,
Then it hid its charms.
Is it shy, or is it sly?
What kind of plant did my mother buy?

Chaemil Rbyn Goodfellow (10)
Lavender Primary School

The Waitress Of Winter

The waitress of winter doesn't serve you
cakes or apple pie or ice-cream slates,
but snowy lakes and plates of snowflakes.
The waitress of winter doesn't serve you tarts
or jelly that does a dance,
but snowy carts and icy parks
because she's the waitress of winter.
The waitress of winter doesn't serve you
meat or pork or lamb or wart-hogs feet,
but sugar coated trees that sparkle in the sunlight.
As she goes to bed
she blankets the ground with a snowy sight.

Natalie Kaye (10)
Lavender Primary School

Getting Dressed

When you're an astronaut and you're getting dressed
you put on your knickers and you put on you vest.
Your spacesuit is gas tight so keeps out all gases.
You put on your back pack and all of your masses.
You put on your boots and helmet and gloves
then you can go up up above.
There's an inner helmet, I forgot that,
it goes, inside your hat.

Emma Bedford (10)
Lavender Primary School

The Freaky Teacher

The teacher walks into the class
Holding her teeth in a glass
Bloodshot eyes, red in the face
She looks as if she's from another race
Opening her mouth, ready to shout
Why is she so mad, what's it all about?
Closing her mouth, deciding not to speak
Everyone's relieved, she's giving us a treat
She strolls into the centre of the room
Her eyes fixed on a wooden broom
Picking it up she looks around
Nobody makes a single sound
Glaring at me, she gives a grin
It's not fair, I haven't committed a sin
Walking towards me, she suddenly exclaims
'Who wants to do cooking, or maybe games?'

Richard Chapman (11)
Pinner Park Middle School

Birthday Post

Early in the morning down our street,
The postman comes on his two flat feet.
He waves to me, I wave to him,
I wonder what he's brought for me.
A book, a toy or a plastic stick,
That would be useful to me.

Jinisha Patel (10)
Pinner Park Middle School

JAMES BOND 007

Now here is a rap about a master spy
A master of disguises was always in the sky.
A stunt man
An action man who has a licence to kill!
Jaws
Doctor No
Goldfinger
There's much, much more
In all the films that he's been in
There's a stunt that's always fitted in.
Explosions!
Fights on a train!
Falling off a cliff!
It's worse than the cane!
Blow up pens
Lazer watches
Parachuting cars
All sorts of gadgets
This guy never gives up!

Paul Murray (10)
Pinner Park Middle School

LAZY CAT

Lazy cat, lazy cat
Anywhere they go they sleep
Zooming across the carpet
Yawn when they're tired
Cats sleep all the time
Anyone they see they hate
They only want to eat mice!

Ban Nasar (10)
Pinner Park Middle School

FIRE

Fire burns like the sun,
In the oven is cooking a bun.
The fire is orange, the fire is red,
At night it is so hot I can't go to bed.

*Fire, fire, big and bold,
It won't go out, it won't go cold.*

Fire is warm,
It's beginning to dawn.
Fire is bright,
It gives us the light.

*Fire, fire, big and bold,
It won't go out, it won't go cold.*

Komal Mistry (11)
Pinner Park Middle School

THE HORROR SCHOOL

Wake up scared to move
Thinking of the horror school,
Oh no! it is Miss Hall
She's the one with big, black, sharp teeth,
And the long black hair to match the big, black teeth.
Then assembly with Mr Long,
He is fat and smells of a nasty pong.
Uh oh PE, Mrs Chunchlod, she could throw you a mile,
Be careful or you'll get piled
That's what I've got today, but what about tomorrow?

Donna Phipp (10)
Pinner Park Middle School

TIME

Time.
You can't turn it back
When you did something wrong.
You can't turn is back
When you made it too long.
You can't put it forward
To see what you'll do.
You can't put it forward
To see your new shoe.
Time goes too fast
Don't waste it, let it cast
Your present and future
Because soon it will stop.

Laura Nicholson (11)
Pinner Park Middle School

BROKEN HEART

My heart is broken because of the pain
you didn't stop to think that it wasn't just a game.
You promised this, you promised that
but you never did come back.
All the lies, all the pain
you're the one who should be taking the blame.
You left me with a broken heart
now there's nothing left in my heart.

Aimee Oram (12)
Pinner Park Middle School

The Geek

Every day of the week,
I see the same old geek,
He picks his nose,
And bites his toes,
And never gets off my back.

He reads a stupid book,
Plus he gives me a funny look,
He's always bare,
And doesn't care,
And plays an out tune bassoon.

It's not that he's got funny eyes,
And not that he always lies,
He's ten and can't even write,
Plus he's not even that bright,
He hasn't got one friend,
And got broken lens,
He is so silly,
And his second name is Billy.

Yusuf Aleem (10)
Pinner Park Middle School

REFLECTIONS

Joy was the eagle who flew high in the sky.
Despair was his mate who watched from her cage.

Patience was the spider who wove the silken web.
Impulse was the boy who ripped it with a stick.

Loneliness was the old man who lived all alone.
Friendship was the child who gave him a smile.

Hate was the bullet that bit into the man's arm.
Love was the doctor who tended to his wounds.

War was the word that made people cry.
Peace was the song that comforted them.

Rose Dykins (10)
Raglan Junior School

RAIN

Splish splosh goes the rain,
Pitter patter against the window-pane.

Dark heavy clouds fill the sky,
While we're inside keeping dry.

Umbrella up and wellies on,
My mum is ready, she's already gone.

Rain please go away,
Please come back another day.

Sarah Boyes (10)
Raglan Junior School

PHOEBE

She turned up
On our door one day
A little puppy
Lost her way.
We took her in
And gave her food
And got her into
A playful mood.
Now she's ours,
Phoebe's her name.
We bought her a collar,
To say the same.
We didn't know
Anything about her,
And now we couldn't
Live without her.

Sam Lindsay (10)]
St Christopher's School

CAUTION

Caution, caution
A Velocirapter is coming
It's fast, it's slow.

Caution, caution
A hungry T-Rex is coming
It's fast, it's faster and hungrier than before.

The Stegosaurus is like a sloth
It eats leaves
It's slow and keeps its pace.

The long necked Braceasaurus
A leaf eating thing
It eats nearly all day.

Ben Tucker (11)
St Christopher's School

ON THE FIELD

As I put the armour on, I was weighed down by metal.
I got onto my horse, I looked up at my opponent in fear.
As I was given my lance I shivered, I was scared.
The referee spoke, 'The Black Knight has challenged thee to a joust.
Do you accept this challenge?'
'I do.'
'Let the joust begin!'
My heart was pounding, it skipped a beat, the horse galloped on.
I held my lance up, suddenly the horse jumped, it was scared too.
It went forward, I looked behind me then an unbearable pain
penetrated deep into my body.
I felt my stomach then I looked at my blood covered hand
dripping with blood.
Then I thought 'The Black Knight has struck.'
I looked at my opponent then the sky, and after that I closed my eyes
and fell limply to the ground like a leaf falling from a tree in autumn.

Ross Kemp (11)
St Christopher's School

AUTUMN

Autumn's in the air,
And it comes to bare,
Of the longer days,
Trees and flowers of their beauty.

Chestnuts, leaves,
Falling from the trees,
All sorts of colours,
Dancing in the breeze.

Gold, yellow,
Purple and brown,
All around makes a
Carpet on the ground.

Autumn's in the air,
And it seems to bear,
All happy things,
Autumn fires, chestnut roasting.

As autumn passes,
The days grow shorter,
The landscape's cold and bleak,
Disappearing in the shadows of the night.

Alexandra Doonan (11)
St Christopher's School

THE PLAYSTATION

My mum just doesn't understand the feeling,
The rush of energy that runs through your arms.
The urge to soar onto a higher level,
It's so very hard to keep yourself calm.

The PlayStation is a waste of time,
But oh what joy it brings.
The sensation when you complete the level,
It's much more fun than anything!

One quarter of my class has one,
And all I've got is a boring Gameboy,
'It's so unfair,' I say to mum,
But all she says is, 'It'll be better in the long run.'

Of all the games of the PlayStation,
Crash Bandicoot 2's the best.
He's a little rat that jumps and spins,
And belly flops his enemies.

So whenever I go over to a friend's house,
(A friend that has this mindless game)
We are always kept amused,
By this simple little object - the PlayStation.

Rebecca Levy (10)
St Christopher's School

MY VERDICT ON THE AUTUMN DAY

I wake up to find that there are no birds singing,
Instead the wind is howling,
And in my bed I lie,
As I say to the summer bye-bye,
But still as the golden leaves fall from trees,
And as I can't hear the annoying buzz of bumble bees,
I think I quite like this season,
But not quite as much as the other seasons.

When I look up what do I see?
A wonderful chestnut tree!
So I look down to see so many conkers,
That I think that I'm going bonkers!
I start to quickly gather them,
Although I don't know what I'm going to do with them.

When I got to bed in the night,
And while I turn off the light,
I change my mind about today,
I think I quite like the autumn day.

Lakshman Harendran (10)
St Christopher's School

TEACHER

Sir Fluke I'm told,
    Is far too old.
He is a nice fellow,
    But his teeth are too yellow.
Unlike Mrs Beech,
    She has perfect speech.
She plays the piano,
    And her voice is soprano.

Mrs Twit,
    Is like an old git.
But I do suppose,
    She covers up the wart on the end of her nose.
Last but not least,
    The most horrible beast.
Mrs Best,
    Unlike her name.
Is tall and dark,
    And most likely insane.

Kathleen Moloney (11)
St Christopher's School

AUTUMN

Autumn, it's the time of year
When the sun has lost its cheer.
Green leaves, they turn to brown,
Not so much greenery all around.
September, October, November too,
There's really very little left to do.
I try to make the best of the situation,
Because you know September,
That's right.
It's the start of a new term's education,
It's time now to knuckle down
Because even though,
Autumn leaves are brown,
It's nearly Christmas, can't wait for that to come around.
I don't mind the wind and the rain,
It's rather nice - a nice warm coat, a hat, perhaps a brolly.
I look around, people are still rather jolly.
Autumn, it's not that bad.

Nico Dontas (11)
St Christopher's School

THERE IS ONLY ONE THING IN LIFE

There is only one thing in life,
that really matters,
to a husband it's his wife,
to a baker it's his batters.

To a child it's her toys,
to most girls it is boys,
to a teacher it's her chalk,
to a queen it's her golden *fork!*

To a pig it's his tail,
to a postman it's his mail,
to a hamster it's his food,
to me it's my brother's bad mood.

To a Polo it's his middle,
to a musician it's his fiddle,
to a mouse it's a cat,
to a magician it's his hat.

To a book it's the pages,
to my mum it's her wages,
to my bike it's the pedals,
to a champion it's her medals.

To a dog it's his bone,
to my brother it's the phone,
to a stallion it's his mare,
to me it's to care.

Nadine Higgin (11)
St Christopher's School

WAR

Why war?
What are we trying to solve?
Why around war
Does the earth revolve?

A single smile
Followed by a million tears
No other smile for a mile
And still war for years.

People pray
For it to go away
Day after day after day
And soon we'll have a peaceful May.

Why the urgent need
For something so strong?
Why need to wait
For everything to go wrong.

The answer to the problem
Is not a gun
Don't deny it:
Something's got to be done.

Stop the pain
Stop the sorrow
Let us go free
For there might not be tomorrow.

Samina Karimbhai (11)
St Christopher's School

SEA SPRAY

The sea is full of fish and
                  Seaweed and
               Shells and
                    Cockles and mussels
                And
                Sea urchins

And
Old boots and
    Glass and
        Paper and
            Sewage and
                Bottles and cans
        and
Plastic bags.
People don't think it's an enormous sin,
To use the sea as a rubbish bin.
Soon the sea will be full to the brim,
Of bottles and cans and bits of old tin.
Can't *they* understand that the sea
Is just as important as you or me.

Joanna Smith (10)
St Mary's RC Primary School

DREAMS

D   rifting on a soft white cloud
R   eady not to hear a sound
E   arthly smell and birds singing
A   ngels flying and keep on bringing
M   agical gifts plays the cello
S   haron comes in and eats gello!

Sharon Entsua-Mensah (11)
St Mary's RC Primary School

SUNRISE

The sun rose up
And a new day dawned
The lion got up
And it growled and it yawned.

The elephant roared
And it lifted its trunk
Then it went down in the water
Like a ship that had sunk

When the snake got up
He looked at the sun
Then he thought of the day
And he hoped he'd have fun

The monkeys of the trees
Started to laugh
And they felt the hot sun
And the cool day draught

The parrot too woke up
And looked at the red hot sun
Then he looked at all the damage
That the species called man had done.

Katie Bermingham (10)
St Mary's RC Primary School

A River

I start at a mountain, a wonderful place
Then I go through woods, fields and bushes, it's really ace

I get bigger and bigger on my way
It's lovely because the sun is out and it's the beginning of May

Then I come to London, a horrible place
People throw litter right in my face

When I'm past that I'm really glad
But my life's nearly over and I'm a little sad

I get faster and bigger on my way
And wait for the last seconds of my life to trickle away.

Sam Hyman (11)
St Mary's RC Primary Schoo

Counting Down To E

40 days to Easter
40 days to go
I can't wait to eat my Easter eggs
all hidden in a row.

10 days to Easter
10 days to go
I can't wait to see what eggs I get
but I've really got to go.

It's Easter day
It's Easter day
Got lots of eggs for after tea
but they're only for guess who? Me.

Laura Moody (10)
St Matthew's CE Primary School

SPACE

Space, the final frontier!
What you are just about to hear . . .
You must reveal to no one!
I am going to tell you about . . .
Mercury, Venus, Uranus, Saturn, Jupiter, Mars, Earth, Neptune
And Pluto.
I'm not talking about the dog Pluto!
Space is a huge place
With dozens of moons, stars and lots of other things.

What I am just about to tell you,
No scientists have covered!
No spaceship has ever seen!
I am going to tell you something . . .
You will find in no book or,
The most highly teached encyclopaedia!
You will be amazed how little effort . . .
It took me to find this information!

What I am about to say is that . . .
I have seen the world!
It was a beautiful sight!
But my brother says I'm crazy!
He says it's just a plastic ball!

Thomas Alner-Newns (10)
St Matthew's CE Primary School

I Am Half English, Half French

I am half English, half French,
Bonjour Madam,
I can speak English,
I can speak French,
And my name is Shalil,
I've seen the Eiffel Tower,
I've seen the London Bridge,
Now all I want to see is the Queen's Palace,
I've seen the Queen's Palace, now I want to see
My pen-pal,
Who lives in Germany.
I've seen my pen-pal,
I want to go to my two houses now,
One in Europe,
One in France,
'Now let's see which I should go to first.'

Farha Ahmed (10)
St Matthew's CE Primary School

Spring

It's spring, it's spring,
Get out your springy gear,
It's spring, it's spring,
Put away your winter gear.

The birds are in
The blossom trees,
Soon there will be lots of fruit,
Like apples, oranges, satsumas.

Busy bees making honey,
So we can have in our tummy,
Lots of lambs are being born,
Foals, piglets, bunny rabbits.

Easter's coming,
Lots of eggs,
Look in the Bible,
And see Lent.

Sophia Tremenheere (10)
*** St Matthew's CE Primary School***

PANCAKE DAY

It's Pancake day,
It's Pancake day,
Dad's cooking pancakes for you and me,
Hurry home from school,
Well I'm on my way home, there's the house, I made it,
I'm getting changed as fast as I can,
There I'm ready to have my pancakes,
Dad does a last toss, it goes up and up and up
and it's stuck on the ceiling,
Oh well, one pancake short, let's eat
And sing our little rhyme, here we go,
1, 2, 3, get your eggs, get your flour,
put them together, it's Pancake Power.

*** Carl Perryman (10)***
*** St Matthew's CE Primary School***

MY FRIEND AT SCHOOL

My friend at school is very tall,
She walks down the long, long hall,
At our school we have a swimming pool,
When she falls over,
Her legs touch the long, long pool,
At the end the teacher calls her
To get out of the swimming pool,
So now you know my friend at school.

Lauren Johnston (9)
Suffolks Primary School

SILVER

Silver looks like a diamond floating in a silky river.
Shines so bright in the moonlight with a darkness.

Shines bright as steel
with a shadow so dark and smooth.

Small and bright as a diamond
shining in the sky at night
so lovely and bright.

Charley Gudgeon (10)
Suffolks Primary School

Your Mind Your Heart, My Eyes

I'm going to fill your mind
with pleasure
I'm going to fill your heart
with love
I'm going to open my eyes
once more
to see the world above.

Shanie Partridge (10)
Suffolks Primary School

White

The shining clouds gloss in my eye brighter than the sun.
The glittery shining seagulls fly past me in a flash of lightning.
The moonlight shines as bright as heaven.
The stars are like a blob of paint.
My big white kite heads towards the silky clouds.

Shaun Howlett (10)
Suffolks Primary School

Summer

The trees are full of blossom,
the sun is shining,
the grass is full of flowers,
the grass is as an apple,
and the people are laying on the beach,
and the children are playing in the sea.

Alex Massey (10)
Suffolks Primary School

Empty Space

Plunging into the silent, eerie blackness of the unknown.
Endless journey through the empty timeless galaxies.
Rushing past glowing diamonds, shiny shooting stars bombing past.
Nebulae, planets spinning past my eyes,
Floating lifelessly like a lost red balloon through the dark gloom
of space.

Dry deserted dusty deserts,
Blowing hurricanes knocking me over.
Arid, colourless, ancient civilisations laughing.
Crumbling beneath my feet.
Cloudy gases, cold landscape.
Spirits watching me.

Elizabeth Proctor (10)
Springfield Primary School

Drifting Through Space

I look outside, nothing there, suddenly I see a comet fire
by leaving a trail of gases behind.
Total blackness as we pass the brilliant bright stars.
We travel thinking about the secrets of black holes, what
happens inside?
Stars sparkle like sailing diamonds in the black pit of darkness.
Blinding beams and rays from the sun stream towards us.
Hurricanes, typhoons, of toxic gases shoot from the ground.
The mystical moons of each planet covered in giant black
creepy creatures.
I look at the crumbly colourless boulder standing in mid-air.

Daniel Fair (10)
Springfield Primary School

MYSTERIES OF SPACE

Deadly silence, empty lonely eclipses likes darkness
Creepy mystifying stars gleaming brightly
Hot metallic comets catapult past at warp speed, crumbling
in a hot cluster.
Caramel moon shining brightly in the darkness
Craters creamy colours, cracks seen clearly
Light rings of gas floating weightlessly around the hot molten
burning planet.
Floating higher and higher into oblivion, waiting to find the
impossible.
Greedy monsters sucking, whirling viciously, waiting to suck you
in deep, deep into nowhere.
Land-breaking silence as we land heavily
Mysterious darkness terrifying eerie galaxy
Warm and cold at the same time, colourless world of dust
deserted landscape.
Bumpy planet, crumbling step after step
Breath after breath.
Boiling burning stars twinkle like diamonds in the silence of this
vivid stratosphere of darkness.
Waiting, waiting to find the extraordinary and eerie wonders of the
place we call space.

Nourdine Arsalane (10)
Springfield Primary School

An Endless Journey

Diamonds twinkling, an endless journey.
Cold, dehydrated, lifeless area.
As I flew swiftly through space, I saw a flying star whiz
past my window.
Stars sparkling, galaxies spinning, moons orbiting planets,
Meteoroids shoot past me.
As I fly in my gigantic rocket, I see a comet speeding past me.
Clusters of diamonds slowly fade away into the darkness.
A giant red ruby, glistening in the sunlight.
Silent, toxic, empty planet drifting in space.
In the distance I see small dark planets, orbiting the enormous sun.
Hot, deserted, arid landscape.
I see amazing sights as I explore this wondrous planet.
Dark, lonely, dry world.
The red fire-ball shines on every planet in the universe.
I speed past planets I see Venus, the planet of love,
With pink poisonous clouds above it,
Like great lumps of candyfloss.

Quynh Vo (11)
Springfield Primary School

A Journey Through Space

Smooth, shiny speeding space shuttle
Speeding into the empty lifeless galaxy,
An endless journey through the eerie unknown,
Rushing asteroids falling through the open atmosphere,
The rocket zooming past nebulae diamonds,
The whole universe full with clusters of gems like a crown of
priceless jewels.

Deserted creepy planets as colourless as a dry desert,
Huge craters bumpy mysterious,
Lost, cold, spooky, just darkness,
Ancient civilisation watching over me,
Arid landscapes, dusty atmosphere,
A whole cluster of cloudy gases.

Chloe Wall (10)
Springfield Primary School

DEHYDRATED, DESERTED SPACE

Silent, dark, mysterious galaxy.
Fast meteorites falling, dripping like rain.
Cold, icy, lifeless, bleak, nippy, frosty area.
Small, shiny stars sparkle.
Gloomy, dim, murky unknown world.
Clusters of spacy stars shimmer in the distance.
Misty, cloudy gases flying through the never-ending black universe.
Dark, sooty evil shadow cascaded over me.
Shooting diamonds, speed away into emptiness.

Deserted, mystifying, arid landscape, incredible vision.
Dark, toxic, creepy, crumbly craters.
Round, icy rings of gases, choking dusty planets.
Tremendous, opening atmosphere.
Bright, ageing moon coming closer into view.
Stars whizzing past bumpy, rock-hard, lifeless planets.
Dehydrated, thirsty asteroids, warping into murky quasars.
Burning, lumpy hills, crumble down silently, and steadily.

Loan Kim Thi Truong (10)
Springfield Primary School

A Journey In Space

Huge, white, shiny rocket with roaring engines makes smoke
like a person smoking.
Small, silver, stars shimmer.
Fast, incredible journey through a deep, black hole in space.
Endless journey through boring darkness.
Bright twinkling stars and unseen comets in the pitch-black
background.
Beautiful see-through diamond sparkles in the night sky.
Lonely, mysterious silence envelopes the dark, gloomy galaxy.
Dry ground, bumpy craters with no sign of life.
Barren and deserted planet which lacks colour and is extremely dull.
There's nothing to do, nothing to see, it's so boring.
Weird planets with huge amazing rings.
Lost, creepy, dusty distant universe, how different from the earth.

Charlotte Dudfield (10)
Springfield Primary School

Space

My round silver-grey metal spaceship
Glides, across the lonely universe.
I see millions of shiny stars,
A massive round blazing sun blinding me.
The empty unknown, secret silence makes me
feel creepy, lost inside.
The vision is one of a cloudy dark mass.
Bright-red balls of fire surrounded by sparks of dust.
The mysterious round planet lost in the massive dark universe.
I walked past the cold, bleak planet
The sky smells like bonfires and fireworks.

Lee Cornwall (10)
Springfield Primary School

DARK SKY

Blast-off.
I seem to feel gloomy.
So dark mystifying planets fading into the distance.
The galaxy large, round, big, bumpy.
All I hear is silence
I see the hard, creepy, lifeless craters.
The bright hot fiery shooting stars zoom across the black giant galaxy.
The hot deserted dusty planets.
Comets fly mysteriously over the moon, gliding through beautiful stars.
The endless never ending constellation shining brightly through the eerie world.

Andraé Michael Barrow (10)
Springfield Primary School

SPACE

Empty, lifeless journey to the never ending world.
Seeing the unknown lonely secret of the diamond sky.
Lost, timeless in the universe to the cold planet.
The timeless journey is over.

I walk past the bleak landscape of the planet.
Looking down the black hole to another world.
The horrifying, crumbly floor, about to cave in.
The dusty, cloudy dark endless planet in the galaxy.

Lauren Wadley (10)
Springfield Primary School

TRIP TO SPACE

There's nothing but silence, lonely and eerie.
Firing stars making their way through space.
Shooting meteorites hitting the moon at great force.
Bright shiny galaxies,
Nothing but planets, stars and spaceships everywhere.
Bite-size diamonds buried in all moons.
Firing comets all over space.
Motors landing on all different planets.
Crash, bang, wallop, they land and walk towards the door.
As it opens, clouds of smoke appear, nothing can be seen.
Rockets flying at bullet speed jumping planet to planet.
We step out of the capsule and float in a most peculiar way.
Stars sparkling and brightening up the atmosphere.

David Howard (10)
Springfield Primary School

IF I WAS...

If I was a landscape I would be a lake which sparkled like the stars in the night sky, when the sun shines down on it.
If I was a fruit I would be a plump and juicy pear which is as cool as the night breeze.
If I was an animal I would be a dolphin as friendly as a puppy and as playful as a kitten.
If I was a colour I would be blue, the colour as deep as the sea and as smooth as a Galaxy chocolate bar.
If I was a flower I would be a lily which stands out from the rest of the flowers and is white and beautiful.
If I was a poem I would be full of adventure and the adventure would end now.

Polly Checker (10)
Trafalgar Junior School

IF I WAS...

If I was a colour I would be yellow
As nice and clear as a bright meadow

If I was a food I would be ham
Or perhaps even a sandwich of jam

If I was a flower I would be a rose
Sprinkled with water using a hose

If I was an animal I would be one of the mice
Nice and easy and I wouldn't have to think twice

If I was a bit of stationery I would be a pen
Nicely writing a boy's name, Ben

If I was a car I would be a Peugeot
Going round and round, not the same as a Renault

If I was a bit of furniture I would be a bed
Nice and warm like I said

If I was an encyclopaedia I would be on a computer
So I would be more intelligent even than a teacher.

Kathryn Sibley (10)
Trafalgar Junior School

MISS WIG

There was an old teacher called Miss Wig,
Who looked rather like a pig,
Her nose was thin, she slept in a bin,
And her favourite fruit was a fig.

Jess Purdue (10)
Trafalgar Junior School

SUPER SOCCER

Soccer is my sport
Soccer is my game
Soccer is a wicked sport
As Arsenal win again
Soccer is bad
Soccer is mad
Soccer is everything
So girls, don't mistake yourselves
As soccer will soon take-over you.
Soccer is good
Soccer is my friend
Soccer is the best sport any boy and
girl can have.

Baljinder Sekhon (10)
Tudor Primary School

A BRIGHT DAY IN SUMMER

The sun is out and shining bright,
With all the light.
The birds are flying high,
Up in the sky in the blue sky.
They are flapping their wings,
While the nightingale sings.
The flowers have shot out,
While children are playing around and about.
The flowers are growing,
And the roses are showing.
People are having ice-creams,
And are having nice dreams.

Nisha Mohammed (10)
Tudor Primary School

MY LITTLE SISTER

I have a little sister,
She can be a little brat.
When she's good she's wonderful.
But when she's bad, she's blunderful.

She scribbles on my pictures,
She makes me late,
She never lets me watch my programmes,
She takes things off my plate.

And when she's good she's wonderful.
And when she's bad she's blunderful.

. . . But I still love her.

Kulvinder Dhaliwal (10)
Tudor Primary School

WATERFALL

A watery grave for the fish,
A refreshing drink for the elephants.
As loud as a hurricane, rushing through the town.
Playful and fun in the red-hot sun.
Sparkling like the moonlight in the dark sky.
Full of weed and other bits that people just throw in.
As dangerous as a dragon, breathing hot fire.
Icy cold in the winter, when Christmas is arriving.
As wet as the swimming pool.
It comes down as fast as Concorde.
If somebody tries to swim in it, they're sure to drown.

Karina Atwal (10)
Tudor Primary School

ALIENS ARE COMING TONIGHT

Aliens are coming tonight
whatever you do.
They've got billions of eyes
whatever you do.
Aliens are fat and greedy
whatever you do.
They have eyes on their heads
whatever you do.
They're slimy and wet
whatever you do.
Aliens are coming tonight
whatever you do.

Jasbinder Nijjar (10)
Tudor Primary School

THE UFO

I saw a UFO.
It was like a big fat toe.
I called the FBI.
They said, ' Please do not cry.'
I saw a big bright light.
They reported that it was weird.
They said, 'Can you be quiet and let us
search our beards.'
I said 'Will you come?'
They said, 'We're busy eating our plums.'

Suchet Bhamra (10)
Tudor Primary School

COMETS

Comets go whizzing by,
In the night, in the midnight sky.
Whizzing round the universe,
Trying to get there first.

Trying not to get too near the Sun,
Going round, having fun.
Going round and round the Moon.
Coming to Earth very soon.

Blazing like a fire-ball,
Making sure it does not fall.
Going in and out the stars,
The next planet's going to be Mars!

Navjit Singha (10)
Tudor Primary School

WATERFALL

Watery, wet waterfall,
Refreshing water, splashing on my face.
Sploshing, wet waterfall,
Thundering water falling down.
Sparkling water in my eyes.
I can hear the dangerous waterfall rushing down.
I can feel the icy-cold water if I stick out my tongue!

Anju Ganger (10)
Tudor Primary School

The Twinkling Stars

The stars are twinkling up so high.
The shooting stars go flying by.
The night sky seems so bright with all those stars' shining light.
I wish I was a star, only gleaming in the dark sky and fading away in the light of day.
If only I could hold the stars and make them mine to play.

Kiranjit Gill (10)
Tudor Primary School

Space

Space is dark.
Space is all around us.
I am rolling through the galaxy.
Bumping into aliens.
Getting a tan by the sun.
Shooting stars rushing past me.
Whoooosh, that asteroid just missed me!

Dale Thomas (10)
Tudor Primary School

Stars

Shooting sparkling stars,
are shining tonight.
White, yellow, blue tonight.
Look a bright silver star,
It seems to be the moon
Or a planet but I can't see it tonight.

Nudrat Rana (10)
Tudor Primary School

THE BEST

Robbie Fowler is the best,
He can beat all the rest.
He beat Beckham in a match,
Schmeichel couldn't even catch!

Everyone had a race,
Andy Cole fell on his face.
McManaman ran really fast,
Ryan Giggs came in last.

Alex Ferguson is dumb,
But Patrick Berger is my chum.
Man Utd are in relegation,
But Liverpool are giving invitations!

Sukhdev Shah (10)
Tudor Primary School

THE MINOTAUR

Half-man, half-bull,
In the labyrinth he stays.
In the dark.
Whoever goes into
The blackness
Never returns.
Then one day Theseus
Went into the darkness
And returned
With the Minotaur's
Head.

Sahra Handule (11)
Tudor Primary School

The Anger of Zeus

Zeus roars loudly
As Prometheus teaches mankind
How to make fire.

When Hera let out a loud cry
In fear of Zeus's anger
Poseidon hears the cry,
As the waves storm
Towards the shore.

Then, as if by magic,
The heavens opened,
A flash of lightning appeared,
And Ares God of thunder,
Stepped out of the stormy clouds.

Then Aphrodite, Goddess of love,
Gave all a potion,
Calming them down.
Mankind was
No longer afraid.

Hushpreet Dhaliwal (10)
Tudor Primary School

The Rocket

I have a rocket in my pocket,
with darkness all around.
With planets and aliens and stars that twinkle.
The stars shoot around and about the moon.
The sun's there too, blazing through space.

Lale Saleque (10)
Tudor Primary School

MEDUSA

Ugly old Medusa
With your two hideous sisters,
And snakes for your hair
Crawling around
Your head and neck.
Slimy old things.
Your heart is
As cold as a stone.

Ashil Waheed (10)
Tudor Primary School

DON'T BE ANGRY

When my mum is angry
She screams
She shouts
'Don't do this!'
'Don't go there!'
'You mustn't do that!'
I run to my room to cry
and weep.
I am filled with fear.
My mum climbs the stairs
stamping her feet and
as red as a tomato.
She bangs furiously on the door.
I don't really hate her
She's the best mum in the whole world!

Gurpreet Mudhar (10)
Warrender School

MY MUM BLAMES ME

My mum blames me
I don't know why.
She says things like
'X!?*- that stupid cat.'
and
'I wish it would X*!? off.'
And when I die
On the last level
Of Rise of the Robots,
I say
'Oh !*-!?'
and she says
'Where did you learn that appalling language?'
And 'cos I like her I say
'At School'
She says
'Well don't say it here'
It's mad.
See what I mean?

Alex Bulfin (10)
Warrender School

TROPICAL STORM WITH A TIGER

The tiger stood, motionless
His eyes like beacons
Watching and waiting
Ready to pounce.

Searching desperately
Through dark-green leaves
A slight growl and whisper
Enter the air.

The lightning flashes across the sky
Like a yellow fork.
The noise, distracting and disturbing
That once again the tiger fails.

The Moon sets
And the sun rises
The brightness shines down
For another day.

Virginia Anne Pilborough (11)
Warrender School

WAR MEMORIAL

There I was
Feeding ducks
When I saw a cross
In the sky
What is it?
I thought
Walking over there
On the road
'It's a *War Memorial!*'
Look at all the
People who've died
In just two wars
'Wow!' It's huge
I'll have a look
For our relations
'Thank God'
No Meehans.

Michael Meehan (11)
Warrender School

WHEN MY MUM IS ANGRY

When my mum is angry,
The house's foundations shake,
You could hear it for miles around,
One kick and the walls buckle,
You can always tell when she's angry,
First she goes quiet,
Then you hear a grinding noise,
Then the walls start to vibrate,
With the yelling,
Soon after you peer out of your hiding place,
You are met by a sweet and nice Mum,
Then you could never tell,
What she was like a few hours ago.

Nathan Mayer (10)
Warrender School

AUTUMN

The leaves are beautiful,
The sky is bright,
The animals are snuggled up,
Ready for the night.

The leaves are crispy,
The sky is dark,
The winds are up,
The wood is stark.

The leaves are golden,
The sky is silver,
The animals look up,
With hearts of wonder.

Bernice Pike (10)
Warrender School

MUM'S HAPPY SPELL

If my mum is happy
She never stops ordering clothes
From her magazines.
She buys loads of sweets,
For me to eat after school,
And she lets me play
On my Nintendo 64 nearly all day.
I wish my mum was always happy
But then an angry spell
Comes along.
And I have to suffer again,
But that's alright,
If I know that she'll
Be happy again soon
And that's what
My mum is like.

James O'Connor (10)
Warrender School

MY MUM

When my mum is angry
Her head goes purple.
And her eyes have long red streaks
coming out of them.
When she shouts I go small
and she gets bigger,
Because she is so loud.
But I love her.

Charley Cox (10)
Warrender School

VARIATIONS

Down behind the dustbin
I met a dog called Jack.
'What are you doing' I said
'I'm going into pack.'

Down behind the dustbin
I met a dog called Ross.
'What are you' I said
He barked, 'I'm the boss.'

Down behind the dustbin
I met a dog called Fred.
'Where are you going' I asked
'I'm on my way to bed.'

Patrick Morris (10)
Warrender School

RAINFOREST

The skies grow dark,
Tail slashing the underbrush,
Growling to himself,
Watching his prey intently,
He pounces,
Screams are heard,

The skies grow darker,
Treading down leaves,
Mumbling to himself,
Eyes like spears set on a target,
He shoots,
Screams are heard and the tiger drops.

Holly Ryan (11)
Warrender School

GUERNICA

Crash!
There was no warning,
The bomb hit Guernica,
Then there was silence,
Later, high-pitched screams and blood,
The Germans had bombed us.

There was no escape,
Screaming and crying,
People in pain,
Suffocating in the small cramped space,
The Germans had bombed us,
Help!

Emma Frankal (10)
Warrender School

SADNESS

Sadness to me
Is missing my grandma
Always full of life
Small with white hair
Brill at drawing
Always sweets by her bed
Wearing a summer dress
Then suddenly
In her sleep
She went away forever.

Sian Roberts (10)
Warrender School

VARIATIONS

Down behind the dustbin
I met a dog called Fred.
I couldn't really stay with him
Because I had to eat my bread.

Down behind the dustbin
I met a dog called Peter.
But my mum called me and said
'Please turn-off the heater.'

Down behind the dustbin
I met a dog called Kim.
When I was about to say something
He saw his friend called Tim.

Aminur Rahman (10)
Warrender School

THE FOREST

There in the forest,
The tiger watches his prey,
Deeply camouflaged,
In the swaying bushes,
Rain coming down heavily,
Lightning striking down fast,
Trees trembling in the thunder,
A tiger, waiting.

Nina Chambers (11)
Warrender School

VARIATIONS

Down behind the dustbin
I met a dog called Kelly.
She hadn't had a bath
And she was very smelly.

Down behind the dustbin
I met a dog called Anne.
When I looked at her
She was sitting in a frying pan.

Down behind the dustbin
I met a dog called Mark.
But when I spoke to him
He started to bark and bark.

Down behind the dustbin
I met a dog called Ross.
He thought he was a boss
Very cross.

Down behind the dustbin
I met a dog called Jade.
She thought that she
Had paid the maid.

Down behind the dustbin
I met a dog called Fred
He was so weak and then
I gave him all my bread.

Christina Western (10)
Warrender School

Tropical Storm With A Tiger

The tiger stood motionless
His eyes like beacons
Fixed on his prey
Waiting, watching ready to get it.

Grace Rumball (11)
Warrender School

I Am The Sea

I am the sea.
Laid-back on some days,
Angry, mad and dangerous on others.
I let people take my treasures.
However, if they take too much they will die
I am generous, yet people still pollute me.
So I break down their sea walls.
Thump!
Thump!
Thump!
I submerge their homes.
They flee,
Now they know my wrath.
I house many beautiful creatures.
They are my family,
Unlike mankind,
They are my friends.

Shyam Pandya (11)
Wembley Manor Junior School

TIGER

I am a tiger,
I have yellowish and black stripes
and my body is really furry.

I have long whiskers and four hind legs,
a large tail and small ears,
and my teeth and claws are sharp.

I am a fierce and strong animal,
I live in the jungle,
where you can find other animals too.

I love to eat zebras and deer,
my favourite part is to suck the bones
at the end of my meal.

Neelam Amin (11)
Wembley Manor Junior School

AUTUMN

Autumn arrives like a golden, green, brown and red nuclear bomb.
It expels the extreme heat that summer has brought.
Autumn escorts gorgeous colours.
It conducts intensively juicy and tender fruits.
Autumn is slowly demolishing.
Everything is getting so cold and frosty.
Winter is coming with his colours.
Beautiful colours are withering away.
Autumn goes to its reassuring resting vicinity.
Where it can rebuilt its energy for next year.

Yannick Wood (11)
Wembley Manor Junior School

TITANIC

Titanic, Titanic the
best at sea
Splish!
Splash!
Splish!
Splash!
Quick and fancy,
Moves so fine,
Like a dolphin
That swims in a line,
A dream that now has
died and drowned.
The ship lies dead underground,
The ghostly wreck of the
Titanic.

Caroline Wyszynski (10)
Wembley Manor Junior School

INSIDE-OUT

Outside

I feel calm and at rest
looking peaceful
not at all bad.
Being nice to all people
All my friends know me
as warm-hearted and gentle.
Can't wait to go to school.

But Inside

Don't catch me in a bad mood
of raging anger
feeling as if I could shout.
Deep, deep down
I want to run away
wild as anything.
Want to get out of class
as soon as school is over
I run home.

Liza Wilkinson (10)
Wembley Manor Junior School

OUTSIDE AND INSIDE

Outside

I am a child
I am a cheerful boy
I always have a lot of strength
In school I feel happy
I never feel sad at school
I'm always helpful

Inside

Inside I feel I'm not free
I'm very sad inside
I feel like a person stuck in a grave
I feel mad inside.

Vishal Sedani (11)
Wembley Manor Junior School

YES MISS

Did you commit crime Miss?
Could you give me a dime Miss?
I saw you kiss Miss?
Why Miss?

I feel dizzy Miss!
Why are you busy Miss?
Miss you look lime!
Miss what's the time?

You're funny Miss
'Cause you have lots of money, Miss
Why is your favourite colour red?
Miss why are you dead?

Shalini Parjan (10)
Wembley Manor Junior School

AUTUMN

Autumn arrives like a person coming from a holiday.
Summer packs its bag and is ready to leave.
It takes with it the clear blue skies.
Autumn brings beautiful tree colours and the animals go into hibernation.
Day by day autumn ages and the leaves drop slowly to the ground.
Three months later autumn returns to Mother Earth.
Allowing winter to return once again.

Nilesh Sikotra (11)
Wembley Manor Junior School

DESTINY

Is it my destiny
not to exist?

My bony fingers reach for air
before I become ensnared.

Will I forever lie
in a pit of my own blood?

Will I be shrouded
in the cold, black space?

Death sings of infinite wisdom and life
Rest.

Will I fall into temptation
and be lost to hell?

Will my body churn and twist
Until I break?
Is my purpose in life never to see the light,
Is this a nightmare?

Rajiv Wijesuriya (11)
Wembley Manor Junior School

THE SUNSET

I love the sunset it has beautiful colours
All reds, yellows, pinks and oranges
I love the sunset it's a beautiful scene
It lasts about two hours but it's just not enough
I wish it lasted all the day because I really love
       the sunset.

Cheri Savary (11)
Wembley Manor Junior School

Hurry Up

Hurry up!
Hurry up!
let's go out to play.
Hurry up!
Hurry up!
it's a nice day.
Hurry up!
Hurry up!
let's go and throw some hay.
Hurry up!
Hurry up
OK! OK! Lets go and play.

Amy Gilbey (10)
Wembley Manor Junior School

Leopard

I am a leopard
Who lives under the hot sun.
Sometimes I go for a run
And I frighten my neighbours.
Some times I sit in a tree
Or run away free.
The sun is so hot I just dive in a pool.
I am as fast as a car.
Sometimes I seem to fly.
I might roar
But deep inside I cry.

Mark Roach (11)
Wembley Manor Junior School

Autumn

Autumn arrives on the stage.
Summer is not strong.
So he packs his bags of blue skies
and warm rays and goes away.
Autumn celebrates in his great autumn festival,
Turning leaves red, brown and many other warm colours
and brings the howling of wind.
Soon he grows weak,
Winter's taking over.
Before autumn goes away,
He says one last farewell.
Winter's taking over!

Kyriacos Papasavva (10)
Wembley Manor Junior School

Autumn

Autumn arrives like a bubble
When it bursts it expands its warm colours.
It chases summer away to where it came from.
It takes the clear skies and the long days with it.
Autumn brings fresh air and grass shiny with dew
Fruits and veg are ready to pick.
Conkers with their spiky shells that drop on the
ground by the brown leaves.
The winter winds blow as it comes closer and closer.

Vijay Tailor (11)
Wembley Manor Junior School

WHAT'S OUT THERE?

What's out there?
I wish I could see
Trapped in this bubble
Wishing to be free.

What's out there?
I do not know
I'm out of the bubble
But don't know where to go.

What's out there?
I have no idea
Things appearing
And they also disappear.

What's out there?
Is it another race?
Trying to figure it out
When it's happening in my face.

What's out there?
I hope I know
But now I can't stay
I have got to go.
What's out there?

Sherida Blenman (11)
Wembley Manor Junior School